CRAVING
GRACE
like chocolate

"The joy of the Lord is
your Strength"
Neh. 8:10

CRAVING
GRACE
like chocolate

How the Gospel Changes Everything

Ruthie Delk

CRAVING GRACE LIKE CHOCOLATE

Illustrated by Deb McCrary
Cover design and book marketing by KevinMcMillan.com

grace - the free unmerited favor of God, as manifested in the salvation of sinners & the bestowal of blessings.

TABLE OF CONTENTS

ACKNOWLEDGEMENTS

This book reflects a group effort. The contents have been shaped by so many people that their fingerprints are literally all over these pages—from dear friends and Bible study groups to a phone call with a stranger.

I am grateful for Mark Bates and Mike Osborne who have given me a steady diet of gospel-centered preaching through the years. Tricia, Alisa, Becky, Karen, and the Co-op Girls, you have been faithful friends, and I laugh when I think of how we have literally talked circles around all of these truths! Thanks for helping me in my journey and being such an encouragement.

To my amazing husband David and children Ryan, Sarah, and Kyle: You are with me on the days when I am living like an orphan and on the days when I am living like His child. You've seen it all and you still love me. Thank you!

Thanks to the CC Smart Mama Bible study for forcing me to write it all down and to dear friends Johnny and Christy Lalonde who in one evening turned a circle into a figure eight. Pure genius!

I am especially grateful to Deb McCrary for using her "doodle skills" to capture the heart of the Gospel Eight diagram. I am so thankful you took "stop doodling" off your New Year's Resolutions list. You have a gift!

To the army of friends who became editors, and to Michelle Damron who led the charge, thank you. You all work fast and on short notice! Couldn't have done this without you!

It is good for our hearts to
be strengthened by grace.

Hebrews 13:9

WHY THIS BOOK?

Since you are reading this book, it means a piece of my heart has found its way into your hands. Frankly, I'm humbled by the thought. My prayer is that this Gospel Eight diagram and the accompanying pages will open your heart to see the gospel in a new way.

There are no earth-shattering truths here. You won't read anything that hasn't been said before by people far more well-read and theologically savvy than I. This is simply the fruit of my journey—a journey where God breathed life into what had become sterile and meaningless to me.

Can you believe that I would say that about the gospel? "Sterile and meaningless?" Twenty years ago those exact words would have perfectly described the impact and importance of the gospel in my life.

At that point I could have recited a list of accomplishments that would have rivaled Paul's in Philippians. I became a Christian when I was a child and was raised in a Christian home (as a missionary kid to be exact—there must be extra points for that!). By the time I was a young adult I knew all the answers and was an expert in keeping pace on my spiritual treadmill.

During high school and college I had a dog-eared copy of *Pursuit of Holiness*, by Jerry Bridges. It was pretty much my bible. I kept copies to give away and was determined that holiness was within reach, if I just tried hard enough.

But while my husband was in seminary (perfect timing, right?), I had a faith crisis that revealed a disconnect between my head and my heart. This agonizing question kept ringing in my ears:

"If **this** is really true then why isn't it making a difference in my life—in how I handle disappointment, how I deal with my pain, how I parent, how I relate to my husband, and on and on?"

I was at the point of spiritual exhaustion. If someone had told me to DO one more thing I think I would have thrown up. **Seriously!** I was so tired of going through the motions, but I was caught on a performance treadmill. I felt completely stuck. I was craving something more. I just had no idea what.

I believed the gospel had the power to change people; it just wasn't changing me. And I was miserable. This disconnect showed up in questions like these:

> If I believed His love was unconditional, why did I feel loved on the days I "got it right" and feel abandoned on the days I "got it wrong?"
>
> If I really believed He was in control, why was I so fearful? If I really believed He was with me, why did I feel so alone?
>
> If I really believed His grace saved and forgave me, why couldn't I extend that same grace to others?

My head was filled with brilliant knowledge about all the wonderful attributes of God, but my heart was not convinced He even knew my name.

During this time, as only God could orchestrate, Jerry Bridges showed up at the seminary to teach on his book

Transforming Grace. David, knowing how much I loved *Pursuit of Holiness* and also how much I was struggling with my faith, encouraged me to attend. I look back now and know without a doubt that God used that class and book to introduce me to grace and breathe life back into me.

Ironically, as I write this Jerry Bridges is days away from releasing his new book, *The Transforming Power of the Gospel*. In an interview recently he says this about his growth in the gospel:

"My first book, *The Pursuit of Holiness*, became a bestseller. But I soon realized that a pursuit of holiness that is not founded on grace and the gospel can lead to a performance mentality and even to discouragement. That's when I began to emphasize grace and the gospel as foundational to the pursuit of holiness."[1]

I desperately needed to be rescued from that performance mentality and discouragement! While I was taking that class, it didn't take long for me to discover that I didn't **really** grasp grace or the gospel. I knew about it in my head but was not experiencing it in my heart. **I felt dead inside.** The truncated gospel I believed in **was** sterile and meaningless. Why? *Primarily because my definition of the gospel was so limited.*

At that time if you asked me what the gospel was I would have rattled off the Roman Road to Salvation or the Four Spiritual Laws or shown you a colorfully beaded bracelet and told you a story about your sin and the solution to it. End of story. That was it. The gospel was simply the entry point. It was the way to begin a relationship with God. Then it was

---

1 http://www.ligonier.org/learn/articles/the-pursuit-of-holiness-an-interview-with-jerry-bridges/

time to go to work. Yes, I believed God saved me, but sanctification—that was up to me.

Over time my definition of the gospel deepened and it changed my view of God as well as my view of sin. An expanding view of God's *holiness*, *love*, and *grace* seeped into my heart and created a growing awareness of my own sin. This made me really uncomfortable, but at the same time revealed what was going on in my heart. I realized I had been making the gospel small. Why?

Because if I didn't need a big gospel or a big Jesus, then I didn't have to face up to being a big sinner. The pattern looked something like this:

When confronted by failure or inadequacy,
I minimized my sin, which led to . . .

↓

Minimizing the holiness of
God, which led to . . .

↓

Believing in a small God, a small Jesus,
a small cross, and a big self.

No wonder the gospel wasn't changing me! As the true gospel became clearer to me, I began to see that:

A big view of my sin led to . . .

↓

A big view of the holiness of
God which meant that . . .

↓

I started worshipping a big God, a big Jesus,
a big cross, and believing in a small self.

When I started sharing what I was experiencing, I quickly learned that I was not alone. I was surrounded by an army of gospel "tweakers." But I also learned that we are not the first generation to water down the gospel. In Galatians 1:6 Paul warns his readers by saying, "I am astonished that you are so quickly deserting the one who called you by the **grace** of Christ and are turning to a **different** gospel—which is **really no gospel at all!**"

Peter says, "So I will always remind you of these things even though you know them and are firmly established in the truth you now have. I think it is right to refresh your memory...see to it that you will always be able to **remember** these things" (2 Peter 1: 12).

This is why I need to be **REMINDED** of the gospel. You do, too. I wouldn't be writing this book if I didn't believe that. We are, as the old hymn states, "...prone to wander, prone to leave the God we love." We need to remember the true gospel—**the gospel that changes everything.**

The first time I heard the phrase, "Preach the gospel to yourself every day," I was dumbfounded. I had no clue what that meant. In my mind I envisioned myself pulling out one of the colorful beaded gospel bracelets and reciting the plan of salvation several times a day. I had a lot to learn. Thankfully God surrounded me with a Christian community and friends that were wrestling with these same issues.

As I grappled with what it looked like in real life to "preach the gospel to myself" I knew I needed a visual to help me understand the tug of war between faith and unbelief that was going on in my heart. How could I make sense out of the way I was living like an orphan and a daughter almost simultaneously? As the diagram in this book evolved, it helped me get a handle on the driving force behind my spiritual schizophrenia.

The purpose of this Gospel Eight diagram and the description that follows is simply to remind us of the gospel. *The real gospel.* The gospel that brings freedom and life and hope. A gospel that is worth celebrating and sharing! *The gospel that changes everything!*

I am especially grateful to family and friends, who have shared with me, cried with me, encouraged me, and challenged me all along this journey. This diagram has been tweaked and modified along the way as every Bible study group has improved it and made it a truer reflection of the cycle of faith in action. I am pretty sure this diagram is not in its final stage. As I grow in my own understanding of the gospel, it will change. *Like any illustration, it can't say everything that needs to be said. It is just a tool to start the conversation.*

My prayer is that this diagram will do for you what it has done for me: give you a clear and concrete way "to preach the gospel to yourself every day." I hope it will help you see how much God loves you, how the cross is the answer to your sin, how His grace propels you on the journey, and how the gospel can bring healing to the hurting places of your heart.

I also pray that it will be a useful resource you can share with others, to show them how Christ really is the answer to everything.

I'm not a particularly avid reader, but a few books and articles have had a profound influence on me. In the pages of this book you'll find traces of Jerry Bridges, Tim Keller, John Piper, Steve Brown and Steve Childers. In the back of this book you'll find a brief list of books and articles that have accompanied me on the journey. Some of them might be helpful to you.

I've also included a few blog posts written by my daughter Sarah that will give you a glimpse of what it looks like to fight for faith in the midst of everyday life.

Let's get started! I can't wait to share my journey with you.

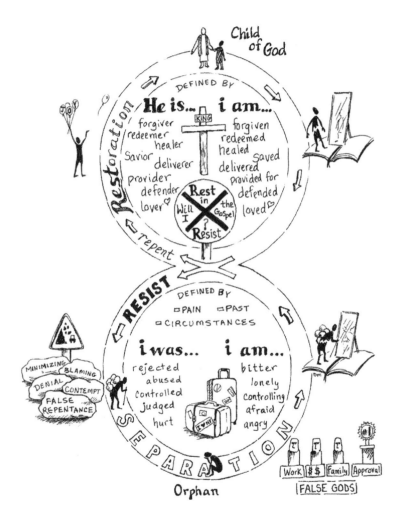

A QUICK OVERVIEW OF THE GOSPEL EIGHT

The **gospel** is the doorway to our salvation, the essential truths we need to believe about Jesus in order to be saved. And yet it is also much, much, more! **It's not just the doorway; it's also the pathway.** It is every promise, every fact, every attribute of God, and everything we need to know, understand, and experience about God and His grace. As described in Ephesians 1, the gospel encompasses **every** spiritual blessing that we have in Christ.

The Gospel Eight diagram reflects what the process of repenting and believing looks like in our lives. Looking at the diagram, you can see that there really is no beginning and no end. Since it's a cycle and a process, anywhere you start will be "jumping in midstream."

But we have to start somewhere, so let's begin with the top part of the diagram that reflects the ideal of a believer's relationship with God. As Christians, we enjoy all the spiritual blessings offered to us in the gospel. As His children, our identity is based on who He is, not who we are. Secure in the Father's love, we delight in sharing with others and inviting them to join the journey.

Even as His children, we fail miserably. If I'm honest, I know that I'm constantly confronted with my inadequacy and sin. Like a mirror, God uses His word, the Holy Spirit, and the community of believers to expose my unbelief and the way in which sin has power over me.

Burdened by this reality, the intersection of the two circles reflects the choice where we decide what we will do with sin. How will I respond when I feel the weight of my sin? I can repent and run to the cross, or, I can resist and turn away from the cross.

In repentance I find full forgiveness that restores me to an intimate fellowship with God. Some have referred to this top portion of the diagram as the Cycle of Faith — a repetitive cycle of repenting and believing, repenting and believing. **This is preaching the gospel to yourself.**

Oh, if only it were this easy! Unfortunately, my heart is easily derailed. Perhaps Satan plants a seed of doubt large enough to make me suspicious of God and His intentions for me. Or maybe I simply mistrust His plan. Or I just feel like I'm not really that bad. For whatever reason, I convince myself that I can handle my sin and my pain on my own.

Although I am aware of my sin and brokenness, I bypass the cross, resist true repentance, and instead head down a path of false repentance that leads me away from God (and into the bottom circle of the diagram).

On this downward path, I develop clever schemes to "manage my sin." From the outside, managing my sin can look like a form of repentance, but it's not. It's false repentance.

False repentance is looking to something else to take away the shame, guilt, and consequences of my sin.

I might do this by blame-shifting, beating myself up, denying my sin, minimizing my sin, or trying to "fix it" on my own by self-effort and trying harder. But all of these lead me further away from God. I feel more and more isolated and separated from Him. I end up living a life that is more characteristic of an orphan[1] than a child.

Instead of finding my identity in Christ and what He has done for me, as in the top circle, my identity as an orphan is defined by my pain, my past, and my circumstances. Life as an orphan robs me of hope, freedom, acceptance, and joy. It leaves me with precisely the life Satan would have me live—one that is disconnected from Christ and spiritually sterile.

As a result, since I've rejected the righteousness that Christ has given me, I strive to establish my own (Romans 10:3). I do this by propping myself up with anything that gives me value and fulfills my need for acceptance. The Bible calls these things idols.

Idols are a cheap substitute for Christ. They may work for a little while, but they all disappoint in the end. At some point I realize that these idols don't deliver and are actually sucking the life out of me. They are driving me further away from Christ and the life He intended. Once again, like a mirror, God's word, the Holy Spirit, and the community of faith help me realize my brokenness and my need for a Savior.

Now I face the same choice. I can run to the cross and be restored through repentance and faith, or resist the cross and continue managing my sin on my own, living like an orphan, and settling for cheap substitutes instead of the real thing.

---

1 Please note that I am not using the term "orphan" to disparage or belittle anyone who has actually lost their parents. I'm referencing the literary/popular definition as those who are forced to live on their own without anyone to look out for them.

As a Christian, this cycle is repeated over and over in my life. As I am confronted with my sin, I can run to the cross, **repent** and believe the gospel or I can **resist** the cross and live like an orphan.

There will be times when my faith is strong, repentance is real, and I live more in the reality of who I am as His child. Then there will be times when my faith is weak, my rebellion deep, and I live more out of my identity as an orphan.

Those outside of Christ are doomed to spin around in the bottom circle desperately seeking ways to manage their pain and brokenness. They crave acceptance and fulfillment but seek it in what the world has to offer instead of finding it in the grace and faith offered through the cross.

This diagram shows both the believer and the nonbeliever that the solution to our despair is the same: we both need to run to the cross!

Recently a friend's Facebook status said, "**If the gospel is not the best news you have ever heard then you have misunderstood the gospel.**" I have no idea of the original source of this statement, but I love it! The gospel really does change everything! It changes my position in Christ, gives me a new identity, allows me to enjoy life as His child, gives me all the blessings and benefits of being in His family, and infuses me with a purpose for living that is greater than myself.

These next few pages will help you understand this process in a little more detail. I hope that as God makes the gospel even more real in your life, this diagram will give you a way to share what you are learning with others.

AWARENESS OF SIN

God always seems to get our attention. Whenever I think I'm doing fine handling life on my own, somehow, someway, He manages to show up and force me to deal with my sin. He's like a full-length mirror that follows us around from room to room. We can ignore it for a while, but eventually we are forced to take a close look and see every flaw and blemish—all the ways we don't measure up to His perfect standard.

That mirror of God's holiness can take a couple of different forms. As my view of God expands, so will my awareness of sin. He will use multiple means to show me my sin. He will expose my unbelief through His **word** (Romans 3:20), through the **Holy Spirit** (John 16:8-9), and through the **community of faith** (Galatians 6:1).

But what is it we are actually seeing in this mirror? If you were to write a definition of sin, what would you say? When I was a teenager, I had a youth pastor who challenged us to go a whole day without sinning. I look back and now realize that he had a very small definition of sin. For him, sin was all about actions. His definition included a lot of "behavioral" words that communicated "not measuring up," "falling short," "disobedience," "rebelling against God," etc.

We prefer thinking about sin in terms of behavior/performance/actions. It's easier that way. It allows me to do two things: I can focus on specific sins and "deal with them." Then when I have cleaned up that area of my life I can move on and work on something else. It keeps things nice and tidy, not messy and overwhelming.

Secondly, if I focus on sin as only a set of behaviors, then it gives me a justified way of puffing myself up. I can usually turn around and find someone who is more messed up than I am. What a relief! Besides, if actions and performance are the only measure, then honestly some days I do okay. You could follow me around and you would see me interacting with friends, spending time with my kids, taking care of my family, and serving others. If sin is just bad behavior, then some days I'm doin' mighty fine!

But sin is about more than just behavior. Our sinful behaviors flow out of a sinner's heart. **We sin because we are sinful.** The danger of focusing only on the external actions is that as long as we maintain a small view of sin, then we will believe in a small cross and a small Jesus. It's a convenient way to keep Him at arm's length.

The result of the Fall is not only that we are separated from God, but that we are also corrupt—tainted through and through. Even our best efforts are still marred by sin.

Let's pretend that I am offering you a piping hot, melt-in-your-mouth Ghirardelli chocolate brownie with added chocolate chips (yum!). There's just one catch. Right before I give it to you I put a drop of cyanide on the corner. Just a drop. You know exactly where it is so you can eat around it. Would you eat it? Probably not. For a large amount of money? Maybe. You might convince yourself that you could break off that corner and still be able to eat a portion of the brownie from the opposite side without being hurt by the cyanide.

That's kind of how we view our sin. *It has just corrupted a piece of us; a corner of my heart, but not the whole thing.* If I am diligent enough I can, with surgical precision, remove the parts that are corrupted by sin, while the rest remains unscathed. What an inaccurate view of sin!

A better analogy would be this: imagine that deliciously thick brownie mixture before it gets poured into the pan. While it is in the bowl I add some cyanide, stir it in, and then bake the brownies. Would you eat them now? No way! The risk is simply too great. The batter has been completely corrupted by the cyanide, and it has worked its way into the entire brownie. Even with surgical precision, there would be no way to extract only the contaminated areas.

This is what we are up against in our battle with sin. It has infiltrated and corrupted every aspect of our hearts. There is no area that has escaped the damaging effects of the Fall. We are completely tainted with sin. It's not just that a part of me is sinful, and so I sin. *I sin because I am sinful.* Sin is so much more than just behavior.

Romans 1 gives us a pretty detailed picture of just how deep the rabbit hole goes, and verses 28-32 point out how desperate we are:

> *Furthermore, just as they did not think it worthwhile to retain the knowledge of God, so God gave them over to a depraved mind, so that they do what ought not to be done. They have become filled with every kind of wickedness, evil, greed, and depravity. They are full of envy, murder, strife, deceit, and malice. They are gossips, slanderers, God-haters, insolent, arrogant, and boastful; they invent ways of doing evil; they disobey their parents; they have no understanding, no fidelity, no love, no mercy. Although they know God's righteous decree that those who do such things deserve death, they not only continue to do these very things but also approve of those who practice them.*

Although any definition of sin would include a list of behaviors like those in this passage, sin goes much deeper than what **we do**. If we miss this, then we put ourselves on a path that will continually keep the beauty of the gospel of grace *just out of reach.*

Romans 14:23 gives us an even broader definition of sin. "Everything that does not come from faith is sin." In other words, *all* sin is rooted in unbelief. We are constantly bumping up against the wall of our unbelief and lack of trust in the gospel.

Our unbelief shows up everywhere, such as when I:
- *listen to lies that say that I'm not lovable*
- *believe that a promotion will solve my problems*
- *turn to food, alcohol, prescription drugs or pornography to numb my pain*
- *work harder to earn God's favor*
- *use excessive dieting and exercise to satisfy deeper cravings*
- *need others to "need me" in order to feel loved*
- *have to control people and circumstances*
- *can't say no for fear of letting others down*
- *am anxious*
- *am critical of others*
- *look in the mirror and hate what I see*
- *demand perfection from my children*
- *live for the approval of others*

Our unbelief is ever-present, and so often we don't even realize it. It shows up in the choices we make, the idols we construct, and the perspectives we have on our circumstances.

In the same way that the gospel **changes** everything, our unbelief **corrupts** everything. If we stop long enough to actually gaze into the mirror, we will find that **we need more than a makeover—we need a heart transformation.**

DIGGING DEEPER

Sin and the Gospel

1. Try to write an accurate definition of sin that includes more than just behavior.

2. What's the difference between viewing the gospel as *just* the 'doorway' of your salvation vs. viewing it as *both* the 'doorway' and the 'pathway' of your salvation?

3. How have you made God small? How does having a small view of God relate to a small view of your sin?

4. God gets our attention through a variety of means. These three were mentioned in this section. Can you think of times when He has used any of these in your life?

   - His **word** (Romans 3:20) to make you aware of your sin?

   - The **Holy Spirit** (John 16:8-9) to make you aware of your sin?

   - The **community of faith** (Galatians 6:1, Matthew 18:15-20) to make you aware of your sin?

5. Just how deep does the rabbit hole go? The answer is sobering. Read and reflect on Romans 1:18-32 and Romans 3:9-20.

6. Take a moment to prayerfully reflect on the sinful attitudes and behaviors that trip you up on a regular basis. Perhaps you are a habitual worrier, or you often experience negative emotions like anxiety, envy, fear, or pride. List as many as you can—and not for the purpose of beating yourself up. Jesus loves you and has paid the price for these sins already. But knowing the pitfalls within your own heart will give you an advantage in learning a new way of repentance and belief.

TRUE REPENTANCE

As God exposes my unbelief and makes me aware of sin, I have a choice. One way to respond is to deal with my sin and failure through the gospel. I can remember what He has done for me on the cross and run to Him with a repentant heart. Repentance means, "I get it, God. I am sick over my sin the same way that You are sick over my sin. I trust You to forgive me and remake me."

True repentance means abandoning myself to the grace of God. It means a full surrender to His love and care. It means that I lean into grace while turning away from the things that have distracted my heart from Him. It means truly resting in His finished work on the cross.

Repentance is hardly ever easy. For me there are often tears and sometimes kicking and screaming. At other times repentance is a quiet letting go. Our repentance is never perfect. None of us will have a heart completely and purely devoted to God in this life. Nor will we be perfectly broken over our sin. But true repentance is the way of the cross—a daily turning away from self-reliance and back toward Him.

I remember one night in particular when God got my attention. David was out of town, and I was at the end of a long week of caring for our three kids by myself. At the time our youngest son Kyle was around three years old and we were muddling through the bedtime routine. (You would think with the third child we would have had it figured out. Nah.) He asked for a cup of water; when I brought it to him he complained that the cup was the wrong color.

Too weary to fight, I dumped the water into a different cup and returned to his room. Let the games begin! He took one look in the cup and asked for more ice. I begrudgingly returned with more ice and then he sweetly informed me that there was too much ice and now it was too cold. Time to start over. This continued for quite awhile. When he was finally satisfied, I collapsed on my bed and with clenched teeth I murmured, "I quit."

Immediately in my heart I heard a response: "You quit too late." At that moment I knew God was talking about more than that bedtime fiasco. He was showing me how independent and stubborn I am. How I cling to my plan until it absolutely doesn't work and **then** I cry out to Him. *I quit too late.*

He is right. Repentance is an admission of how I live independently from Him. Repentance now meant that each day would start with a new phrase running through my head. "I quit Lord; I can't do this without you." This was a huge turning point and a baby step in the direction of learning to live a life of dependence on Him.

My favorite passage is Isaiah 30:15. This will be the first of many times that I mention it. I love it because it so accurately depicts my need for Christ, as well as my resistance to doing life His way. "In repentance and rest is your salvation; in quietness and trust is your strength, **but you would have none of it**."

True repentance takes me to the root of my unbelief. So often I repent of the "fruit" of my sin—things like anger, pride, jealousy, and discontentment. I don't even consider the unbelief that has caused those sins to take root in my life—believing He doesn't love me, that He isn't in control, that He won't provide, etc.

In repentance, these lies are exposed and abandoned. I will battle these lies daily! So daily repentance means that I need to first recognize when I am listening to those lies, and then confront the lie with the truth. Of all the things on your list of things to do today, that just might be the hardest one of all!

True repentance begins with a humbled heart of confession that leads not only to a transformed heart, but transformed attitudes, behaviors and relationships. When I repent, I find the freedom to seek forgiveness and restoration with those I have wronged. Through His Holy Spirit I find the strength to abandon destructive behaviors and replace them with "fruit in keeping with repentance" (Matthew 3:8).

Repentance is a gift that God gives us through His spirit. He convicts me of sin and points me to Christ. Conviction will "look" different depending on how God is trying to get your attention. He might make you sick over your sin, or just restless and grumpy, but one way or the other conviction sets in. The goal of conviction is to take me to the cross and straight into the arms of Jesus. There I am forgiven and my relationship with God is restored. When Jesus said, "It is finished," He meant it! "Therefore, there is now no condemnation for those who are in Christ Jesus" (Romans 8:1).

This journey into repentance requires humility, sacrifice, and maybe even suffering. This diagram reflects repentance as an upward turning which will feel like death. Yet it will lead to life. What a perfect picture of how the gospel turns evil on its head and brings beauty from ashes—all because of the death and resurrection of Christ!

FALSE REPENTANCE

O n many days I would rather do anything than swallow my pride, confess my sin and run to the cross. I would much rather ignore the gospel, bypass the cross, and resist the grace, love, and forgiveness of Christ. Basically, I reject what I am craving—His grace—and head off on my own.

As I cruise away from the cross, I'm left with the question of how to deal with my sin and the conviction that weighs on me. I still know that I am falling short. I know that I am broken inside. I know that I'm bringing destruction into my life and the lives of others. So what do I do?

I see it as a challenge: How will I get out of this? Through this? Around this? Maybe you respond in the opposite way—you crawl in a hole and hate yourself. Either way, **it's amazing how much we can make managing our sin look like repentance.** Don't be fooled—it's absolutely not!

I'm an expert at this. I can even fool myself. I often think that I am "dealing with my sin." After all, I feel bad; I'm really sorry that a situation brought pain to people; I wish things were different, etc. But instead of fleeing to the cross and admitting my sin, I try to deal with the issues on my own. This is false repentance.

Here are some of the common techniques I've used:[1]

- **Blame-shifting:** My sin isn't as bad if I can show that someone/something else is the real problem. "If you knew what I've put up with for so long, you'd be angry too."

- **Just "Fix It":** My sin isn't so bad if I can figure out a way to prevent it in the future. "Here's the plan. Next time this happens here is what I am going to do…"

- **Beating myself up (contempt):** I will really be taking sin seriously if I allow it to make me feel terrible. "I always make the same mistakes. I never get it right. I don't deserve to be loved."

---

1 Adapted from *The Gospel Centered Life* by World Harvest Mission

- **Minimizing:** My sin won't be as bad if I can compare it to other things that are much worse. "Yelling one time after dinner is not that big of a deal compared to how badly the kids have behaved today."

- **Denial:** My sin isn't bad if it's not even sin. "Everyone struggles with this. It's just part of being human."

- **Trying Harder:** My sin will be manageable if I apply myself and work on the problem areas. "I'm going to learn to be more patient and not get uptight when things don't happen the way I want them to."

- **Getting Defensive:** (Does this really need an explanation?)

Do any of these sound familiar? Imagine that one of the bathrooms in your home has gotten completely out of hand. No one has cleaned it in months. (Welcome to my world!) How could you respond?

- You might start by blaming other family members for the messes they have made.

- You could bravely jump in there armed with a bucket of Clorox and rubber gloves. (Scrubbing Bubbles got nothing on you!)

- You might be tempted to sit on the floor and cry because you are such a failure and can't even manage to keep a bathroom clean.

- You could walk in, look around, pick up a towel off the floor, flush the toilet, spray everything with Lysol disinfectant and then walk out thinking, "I've seen worse."

- You could just put a big sign on the outside of the door that says, "Out of service until further notice!" and walk away.

When it comes to sin and our hearts, all of these are examples of false repentance. We are **totally incapable** of fixing our brokenness. A cheesy way to say it would be, "The only way out is to surrender and allow Jesus to 'clean the bathroom'." Cheesy or not, the reality is He's the One who restores our hearts from the inside out.

The reason I love Isaiah 30:15 so much is that it tells me the truth about myself. It tells me the source of my salvation and strength and explains how I refuse it. False repentance is a fake attempt at dealing with my sin. It's insidious and destructive. The scary thing is that it often 'looks' like righteousness. But most of the time we don't realize it. While sometimes looking and feeling like true repentance, it actually leads me farther away from the cross and away from Christ. Jesus encountered false repentance with the Pharisees and called them out in the strongest way possible.

"Woe to you, teachers of the law and Pharisees, you hypocrites! You are like whitewashed tombs, which look beautiful on the outside but on the inside are full of the bones of the dead and everything unclean. In the same way, on the outside you appear to people as righteous but on the inside you are full of hypocrisy and wickedness." (Matthew 23:27-28)

I can always tell when I have fallen into the trap of false repentance. It feels like I am free-falling, relying on myself as the solution to my sin instead of the cross. The result is further separation from God and deeper and deeper cravings.

True and False Repentance

1. Luke 18 includes both parables and individual encounters with Jesus. We get a glimpse into the hearts of six types of people: a widow, a tax collector, a Pharisee, a group of children, a rich man, and a blind man. Which of these people can you relate to? What do these exchanges teach you about humility, performance, and repentance?

2. Which type of false repentance do you typically rely on to manage your sin? (These are just a few...there are many more, trust me!)

    -   Blame-shifting
    -   Denial
    -   Fix-it
    -   Trying Harder
    -   Self-contempt
    -   Getting Defensive
    -   Minimizing

3. What are some of the signs or indicators that let you know God is trying to get your attention and convict you concerning your sin?

4. Do you remember a time when you experienced true repentance? What led to this, and how did it feel? How did you see repentance impact actions and relationships?

5. In your own words describe the difference between true repentance and false repentance. What is the source for each?

JOY

Restoration

DEFIN...

He is...

forgiver
redeemer
healer
Savior
deliverer
provider
defender
lover ♡

King

Rest in

Will I

re
hea
del

p

RESTORATION

True repentance takes me to the end of myself and to the cross. It leads to restoration and renewed intimacy with God. The sin that separated me from God has been dealt its final blow on the cross. Jesus has given me a completely new life in Christ, and also a new identity. I am not the same.

Let's take a closer look at what restores our relationship with God. As Jesus hung on the cross He took on the role of the sacrificial lamb in the Old Testament. He takes on our sin and the resulting separation from God for us. He endured the punishment that I deserved. While He hangs and bleeds, separated from His Father, God pours out His wrath on His only son. God's anger burned against sin. But it also burned against *my* sin—my very real particular sins of anger, jealousy, gossip, criticalness, arrogance, insensitivity, idolatry, and more. The rebellion that boils in my heart today was laid on Jesus, and He took the punishment that I deserve.

If God *poured out* His wrath, then it means **there is no more wrath left.** He is not angry with me anymore. **When I repent, He welcomes me home with open arms.** He throws a party (just like the father did for the Prodigal Son in Luke 15). That's why just before Jesus died on the cross He was able to say, **"It is finished."**

Jesus endured the wrath of God *for us*, but He also *gives us* His righteousness. **This transaction takes us from being objects of His wrath to being recipients of His grace.** It restores our relationship with God and gives us a new identity.

"Like the rest, we were by nature deserving of wrath. But because of his great love for us, God, who is rich in mercy, made us alive with Christ even when we were dead in transgressions—it is by grace you have been saved" (Ephesians 2:3-5).

Imagine you owe a bank one billion dollars. (Now that's a shopping spree!) Think how it would feel if a friend came to you and said the debt is paid. Then she opened an envelope from the bank and showed you an account statement that clearly indicated you owe nothing. That would be unbelievable, and you would feel an incredible burden lifted from your back.

But that still wouldn't mean that you have money to pay the mortgage, or that you would not go into debt again in the future.

So imagine that same scenario with a slight twist. Your friend shows up with the account statement and tells you that the debt is paid. But when she shows you the statement, instead of simply showing a balance of zero, the account shows that you have a balance of one hundred billion dollars! Now that would be overwhelming! You would never have to worry about money again.

But your friend tells you it gets even better. Not only does the account have one hundred billion dollars in it today, but it also will always have one hundred billion dollars in it. No matter how much money you spend, every morning the balance in the account is one hundred billion dollars. It's like a billionaire's *Groundhog Day*!

That's what happened on the cross. It wasn't just that the debt of our sin was paid by Christ, but that we also received His **infinite righteousness.** When we were united with Him in His death, we were also united with Him in His resurrection. God looks at you and sees the righteousness of His Son—a righteousness that will never fade or "run out."

Consider these verses:

> "God made him who had no sin to be sin for us so that in him we might become the righteousness of God" (2 Corinthians 5:21).

> "But God demonstrates his own love for us in this: While we were still sinners, Christ died for us. Since we have now been justified by his blood, how much more shall we be **saved from God's wrath through him!**" (Romans 5:8-9).

"...we have been made holy through the sacrifice of the body of Jesus Christ once for all" (Hebrews 10:10).

"...he has reconciled you by Christ's physical body through death to present you holy in his sight, without blemish and free from accusation" (Colossians 1:22).

This transaction, where He takes my filthy rags and in exchange gives me His robe of righteousness, is what changes me. It changes our position before God and gives us a new identity as His children, clothed in His righteousness. **This is why the gospel changes everything!**

Restoration breeds hope, joy, and freedom. It's the promise that one day, in spite of my circumstances or my pain, God will make all things new. Sometimes when I read my Bible I write down verses that stand out to me in a little journal. One day I was skimming through Isaiah chapters 41-46 and wrote down this string of verses. They are in no particular order, and this is taken straight out of my journal.

Do not fear, I am with you. I have called you by name, you are mine. Remember these things, for you are my servant. I have made you. I will not forget you. I have swept away your offenses like a cloud, your sins like the morning mist. Return to me for I have redeemed you. I will lead you by ways you do not know, along unfamiliar paths. I will guide you. I will turn darkness into the light before you and make the rough places smooth. I will not forsake you. I will pour water on thirsty land and streams in the dry ground. I will pour my Spirit on your offspring and my blessings on your descendants. Forget the former things, do not dwell on the past. See I am doing a new thing. I am making a way in the desert. Even to your old age and grey hairs I am He. I am He who will sustain you. I have made you and I will carry you.

I go back and read this often as a reminder to anchor my hope on the restoration and redeeming work of Christ. Because of the resurrection **He will make all things new!** This gives me hope, especially on those days when I am either discouraged by my sin, or overwhelmed by the pain swirling around those I love, or grieving over relationship that are not working. I long for the day when all of these things will be made right. I know it is coming!

SEPARATION

In the same way that true repentance leads to restoration and intimacy with God, false repentance leads to separation, isolation, loneliness…and idolatry.

In our efforts to manage our sin we are really striking out on our own and leaving God behind. When we do this we're rejecting both Christ's forgiveness and His righteousness. So we don't get to experience the **forgiveness** that comes from true repentance ("There is therefore now no condemnation for those who are in Christ Jesus"), and we also don't receive the **righteousness** that comes through Christ ("God made him who had no sin to be sin for us so that in him we might become the righteousness of God").

We are left empty in all the ways that really matter. We respond to our **guilt** in the only way we can outside of Christ;

by managing our own sin through false repentance. And we respond to our **emptiness and lack** by trying to create our *own* righteousness through idolatry. This sets us on a course of craving *something* to fill that emptiness.

When Paul wrote about the Israelites' dedication to works and performance, he said, "Since they did not know the righteousness that comes from God and sought to establish their own, they did not submit to God's righteousness" (Romans 10:3).

This is crazy talk! Did you catch that? They rejected the righteousness that Christ willingly gave them and settled for their own man-made righteousness. That's like stiff-arming God and saying, "No, I'm good. I got this." *Really?*

Several years ago one of my friends, Kelly, was a single mom juggling a career and two children on her own. (I wish you could hear her whole story—a beautiful one of brokenness and redemption.) During this time, her teenage daughter was really struggling with the rejection of her father and attached herself to a rough group of kids. She had run away before but this particular time they had no idea where she was, and it had been several days. Here is an excerpt from the email she sent when her daughter finally came home:

> She is home. She was dirty, tired, hungry, angry and belligerent but physically intact and arrived on her own accord…or more accurately arrived by God's good mercy and on the breath of your prayers.
> I don't know where she went or what happened while she was gone for 4½ days and there is still no clarity on why she ran away. She is angry and wild-eyed. She said very little to

me and I to her. She almost went into a fit of anger when I told her we were worried and we loved her.

While she showered I prepared a meal that she typically likes, although she was extremely hungry, she refused it and would only eat some pineapple out of a can. We have a feast of love for her but yet she is satisfied with the crumbs. She has rejected again any display of kindness or love. In the midst of this heart wrenching experience I have a moment of clarity. I can't help but see the parallelism—my dearly beloved daughter, for God knows what reason, is refusing our love. I do the same with my Heavenly father in my own walk, if you can call it a walk—more like stumbling, with God. He prepares a feast for me and I refuse to come to the table!

This story still touches me today. I guess it's because I'm so much like her daughter. God has given me *everything* in Christ—His righteousness, forgiveness, grace and love—a feast of everything I am craving. And I have the nerve to saunter by, open a cabinet, grab a can of pineapples and say, "No, thanks. I'm good."

But that is *exactly* what we do—all the time. Instead of clinging to the righteousness of Christ and the worth He gives us, we set off to establish our own worth. We find ways to make ourselves feel competent, successful, happy, distracted, and satisfied. Unfortunately, these efforts always fall short and we are continually on the lookout for the next thing. The reality is when I reject what Christ offers, I have to turn to *something else* to stop the craving.

It reminds me of when it's the middle of the day and I am on the hunt for some chocolate. Any will do. Honestly, I'm not that picky. Actually I take that back. I'd prefer a Reese's or M&M's, but if we don't have those I'm not ashamed to admit that I'll settle for the chocolate chips that I have in a container stored in that useless cabinet over the microwave. I don't need to eat the whole bag, a handful is enough and then I'm set—for a while.

An idol is any substitute for Christ. It's the handful of chocolate chips instead of the Godiva Pearls. It's something that we *hope* will do for us what only Christ can do. Idols never fully satisfy. That's why John Calvin called our hearts "idol factories." It seems like there is always one on the conveyor belt.

What do you run to? What do you crave? Probably not a can of pineapples or a handful of chocolate. **What makes you feel like you have arrived when you get it right or full of despair when you get it wrong?** That's a good place to start when thinking about your own idolatry.

Volumes have been written on this topic, and there are incredible books and Bible studies available to help you get an accurate picture of your heart and the form your particular idolatry takes. If this is your first encounter with the idea of idolatry, I really encourage you to dig deeper into some of those resources. I also want to remind you that this is a process, and sometimes not an easy one. We spend our whole lives trying to cover up what is really going on inside. So to peel back a layer—even one or two—can be a slow and painful process. Be patient with yourself and what the Spirit is trying to show you. You are not taking this journey alone.

Here are some diagnostic questions to help you begin the process of discerning what your own idolatry looks like. One or two of these questions will probably resonate with you and help you uncover your idol.[1]

- *What is my greatest nightmare? What do I worry about the most?*

- *When I go to bed, what is my consuming thought? When I wake up what is my consuming thought?*

- *What do I rely on or comfort myself with when things go bad or get difficult?*

- *What, when I don't get it, causes the most conflict in my marriage and relationships?*

- *What prayer, unanswered, would make me seriously think about turning away from God?*

- *What makes me feel the most self-worth? What am I the proudest of?*

- *What do I crave, that without it, I am miserable?*

- *What do I consistently complete this sentence with? If only I had _____, I'd be happy.*

Here's a peek inside my heart. When I go to bed at night I am typically thinking about one thing: *What did I get done today?*

---

1 Adapted from Redeemer Presbyterian Church's study on Galatians by Tim Keller.

If it's been a "good day," I will have been really productive and efficient and served and loved others well.

If it's been a "bad day," I will have had lots of interruptions, accomplished nothing, and still have a long "To-Do List" waiting for me in the morning.

Can you guess what I'm thinking about before my feet hit the floor in the morning? Brilliant. You got it on the first try. I'm thinking about one thing: *What do I need to do today?*

Do you see what this reveals about my idolatry? It revolves around work, performance, accomplishment. It exposes where I get my value from and what I cling to as the source of my strength. It shows me more about my heart than I really want to know. But it is the scary truth.

What consumes your thoughts before you go to bed and when you first wake up in the morning can tell you a lot about your heart.

You know what else can tell you a lot about your heart and your idolatry? Your anger. *What makes you angry?*

I get angry when I can't get things done. I get angry when constant interruptions keep me from staying on task. I get angry when other people (as in my husband and kids) don't help me get things done around the house. The White Witch in Narnia has nothing on me when I want to get something done and no one wants to help. I need other people to feed my idolatry and when they don't, I get angry. My anger reveals my idolatry.

Idolatry is based on lies—lies about many things, but mainly lies about God. Somehow I have latched on to the lie that I am only worthwhile when I am productive. At some level I believe that God loves me more when I am busy. A deeper lie beneath that is that being productive makes me feel in control. I desperately need to be in control, because I believe He is not. Lies. They are all lies. These lies feed my idolatry and keep me away from God.

I love Isaiah 44. It is too long to insert here but I would encourage you to read it. The prophet is taking aim at the whole system of idol worship and mocking a blacksmith who creates idols. He goes into detail about how he crafts an idol—and emphasizes that it comes from the same piece of wood used to build a fire and bake bread.

"All who make idols are nothing, and the things they treasure are worthless. Those who would speak up for them are blind; they are ignorant, to their own shame....**He feeds on ashes, a deluded heart misleads him; he cannot save himself, or say, Is not this thing in my right hand a lie?**" (Isaiah 44:9-20).

Idol worship is based on believing lies. Lies about God—that He won't provide, or satisfy, or be faithful. Lies that He doesn't love me, He isn't good, or He doesn't care. I often recognize the idol in my heart and try to repent, but I don't go deep enough to see the sin beneath the sin. For example, I may repent of my idol of approval but not repent that I don't really believe God loves me—which is the lie that is causing this idol to grow in my heart.

As idols expand in our hearts they demand to be fed and worshipped. Feeding our idols becomes a full-time job that moves our hearts further away from the only One who can really satisfy—Jesus.

When our idols are exposed, our tendency is to respond with false repentance. We try to manage our sin and run damage control from the fallout of our idol worship. We tend to work hard, or try to "get better" to solve our problem.

Once again, the only real solution to our idolatry is to repent and believe. Repent of the unbelief that lies beneath the idol. Repent of the damaging effects of our idol worship. Run to the cross and Rejoice! Rejoice that Jesus has given you EVERYTHING you are craving and longing for. He has already done it. He satisfied your need and made up for what you lack. You no longer have to reach for the can of pineapples or hold on to that lie.

In the book of Jonah, just before being belched from the belly of a whale, Jonah knowingly proclaims: *Those who cling to worthless idols forfeit the grace that could be theirs* (Jonah 2:8).

Do you know what scares me most about my idolatry? *Clinging to my idolatry takes me further away from grace.* It makes me more reliant on myself and less reliant on Him.

DIGGING DEEPER

Restoration and Separation

1. Read Ephesians 1 and make a list of all the spiritual blessings you have received in Christ. Your list will give you a great start in expanding your definition of the gospel and your view of God.

2. How would it change you, if you really believed that God poured out his wrath on Jesus? (And that means there is no more wrath left to pour on you!)

3. Based on the answers to the diagnostic questions on page 41, what do you think are the idols of your heart? As you name those idols, consider what lies you believe that have given room for these idols to grow.

4. How does clinging to your idol 'prop up your righteousness?'

5. In what ways is your specific idol a corruption of a God-given desire and longing? How does Christ meet that particular need?

6. Read Isaiah 44 and Jonah 2. What do these passages teach you about idolatry?

So much has been written on the issue of idolatry, but here are two of my favorite quotes for you to ponder:

"An idol is the thing you get your identity from and the thing you're turning to for your righteousness. It is anything more important to you than God, anything that absorbs your heart and imagination more than God, anything you see to give you what only God can give."[1]

"Mankind's root problem is not merely an external, behavioral problem—it is an internal problem of the heart. Paul believed that one of the primary reasons human hearts are not more transformed is because the affections of people's hearts have been captured by idols that grip them and steal their hearts' affection away from God (Ephesians 5:3-5) The reason why you commit a sin is because you don't believe God is first, and that He will provide for you."[2]

---

1 Tim Keller, *Counterfeit Gods*, page xvii
2 Steve Childers, "Spiritual Formation Lectures"

LIVING AS HIS CHILD

The insidious thing about sin and the human heart is that what we worship will eventually define us. Over time, the decisions we make about true and false repentance will shape who we think we are—our identity. The cycle then continues, because who we are determines much of what we do. **That is why it is crucial to understand our true identity—because eventually it will impact everything about us.**

Two of our children ran track in high school. One day after practice, their coach had the athletes do an interesting exercise. He asked them to make a list of all the roles they currently had to fulfill—like student, runner, athlete, etc. He then said, "In a few years, many of you will be doing very different things and playing different roles. If you get your identity from what you do, what happens when you aren't doing it anymore?"

Good question. So often we let our identity be shaped by our season of life and our circumstances, both of which are fleeting. Your identity is who you are, not what you do. It's what defines you. It determines your perspective on your circumstances, your choice of actions, and your view of the future. **Getting your identity right is absolutely crucial to really getting the gospel.**

Consider what happened in the Bible when people encountered God. We see all sorts of examples of radical transformation. Scripture is full of stories that show us people whose identity was completely changed by an encounter with God:

- Moses from a rural shepherd to a challenger of kings

- Hannah from a barren woman to the mother of a prophet

- David from a shepherd boy to a slayer of giants

- The Samaritan woman from an adulterer to a disciple

When *we* encounter God through repentance and restoration, we get a renewed sense of who we were made to be and who we are as children of God. We are given a new identity and transformed from:

- Ashamed to unashamed
- Unforgiven to forgiven
- Slave to free
- Enemy to friend
- Unknown to known
- Broken to healed
- Orphan to child
- Unloved to loved

How crazy is this!

> "When we were children, we were in slavery under
> the basic principles of the world. But when the time
> had fully come, God sent his Son, born of a woman,
> born under law, to redeem those under law, that we
> might receive the full rights of sons. Because you are
> sons, God sent the Spirit of his Son into our hearts,
> the Spirit who calls out, 'Abba, Father.' So you are
> no longer a slave, but a son; and since you are a son,
> God has made you also an heir" (Galatians 4:3-7).

So with this transaction on the cross not only are we
forgiven, declared righteous, and given every spiritual
blessing in Christ (Ephesians 1), but we are also adopted into
His family and given the full rights of an heir. **To be forgiven
would have been amazing enough. But to be family? That
is the icing on the cake!** That's why J.I. Packer calls our
adoption, "the apex of our salvation."

Just this week I was listening to Christine Caine, from
the non-profit organization A21 that fights for the end of
human trafficking. She shared how her parents sat her down

one day to tell her that she was adopted. She was 33 years old. I can't imagine how that could wreck your world as well as your view of yourself, your family, and your identity. But what struck me most about her story is what she found on her birth certificate. Instead of her name, she was given a number, and in the description it said, "unnamed."

But all that changed when she was adopted.

Every adoption story I have ever heard involves a story of loss and restoration. The same is true for us. The Scriptures brilliantly portray this in numerous places. But my favorites are in Ezekiel 16 and Romans 9.

Ezekiel 16 is an allegory of unfaithful Israel which is depicted by telling the graphic story of a child that was abandoned at birth. "No one looked on you with pity or had compassion enough to do any of these things for you. Rather, you were thrown out into the open field, for on the day you were born you were despised." Thankfully the story does not end there. "Then I passed by and saw you kicking about in your blood, and as you lay there in your blood I said to you, 'Live!'" The next few verses describe the tender love and care God takes in raising this child and how she grows into a woman whose fame and beauty spread among the nations.

Here's the kicker in verse 15: "But you trusted in your beauty and used your fame to become a prostitute." The remainder of the chapter goes into the sordid details of her wanderings. Then we finally get to the end of the chapter where it says, "So I will establish my covenant with you, and you will know that I am the Lord. **When I make atonement for you...speak of your sin no more.**" What grace! What love! What a story of adoption!

In Romans 9 we find another picture of adoption and an amazing declaration. It's found at the end of a difficult chapter where Paul teaches about the sovereignty, judgment, and mercy of God. Strangely, it closes with this picture of rejection and redemption:

> "I will call them 'my people' who are not my people; and I will call her 'my loved one' who is not my loved one, and, it will happen that in the very place where it was said to them, 'You are not my people,' they will be called 'sons of the living God'" (Romans 9:25-26).

Paul is referencing a passage from the Old Testament, Hosea 1:10. To understand the full significance of this for our identity, we need to briefly review Hosea's story.

God tells Hosea to marry a harlot and then have children. Each child gets a name that displays Gods displeasure and judgment with the people of Israel. Hosea's third child gets the name Lo-Ammi, which means "not my people."

So what does God do in the gospel? He **reverses** that judgment on the people and in Christ fulfills the promise. **"They will be called sons of the living God."**

This is the kind of love and grace we have been enveloped in. It *is* amazing grace! Because of Jesus, our relationship with our Father is restored so we can live as His children.

> "To all who receive him—to those who **believe** in his name he gave the right to become children of God" (John 1:12).

With God as our Father, we have been given a new identity in Christ. Your identity is directly tied to who He is and what He has done for you, not what you can accomplish. **There is nothing left to add; He has done it all.** Here's an equation that shows how our identity as a child flows from the character of God:

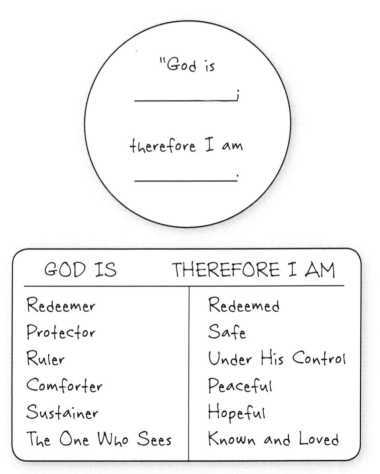

"God is

_____;

therefore I am

_____.

GOD IS	THEREFORE I AM
Redeemer	Redeemed
Protector	Safe
Ruler	Under His Control
Comforter	Peaceful
Sustainer	Hopeful
The One Who Sees	Known and Loved

He is. I am. As His child, my identity is hidden in the eternal love and steadfastness of Christ. My identity is defined by who He is—*not* who I am.

My new identity as God's child results in a chain reaction that eventually changes everything about me; how I view myself, my sin, my circumstances, my pain, even my ministry and service. **This is why the gospel changes everything. Once it gets a hold of my heart, the trickle-down effect is endless...**

- I will have a personal ministry, but not out of my own strength or sense of duty. (No spiritual treadmill allowed here!) Instead I will serve out of a response to what He has done for me.

- I will continually see myself as both a saint and a sinner, clothed in His righteousness but desperately in need of His grace.

- I will view grace as not only what saves me, but what sustains me. His grace begins and finishes the work in my heart.

- I will risk loving others without fear of rejection or hurt.

- I will be able to extend to others the grace He has extended to me. I will refuse to carry a critical spirit into my relationships.

- I will not demand for my idol to be fed. Instead I will see that my idolatry represents a deeper longing and I will turn to Christ to meet that need and thank Him for being enough for me.

- I will forgive those who have hurt me. I can do this based on full understanding of how their sin against me will be paid for one way or the other— either they will trust in Christ for forgiveness or they will spend eternity separated from Him. Either way, I no longer have to extract payment from them.

- I will not be bitter about my circumstances. Instead I will view them as being sifted through the hands of a loving God. There is no Plan B. This is Plan A.

- I will not fret. God is in control. He is capable of caring for me even when I do not understand His ways.

- I will rest in His perfect love for me.

This list is just the beginning but you can see how once the truth of the gospel seeps into your life it _____ everything! (Thought you might have caught on by now.)

I have seen this in my own life. The gospel *has changed* me, *is changing* me and *will change* me! Nowhere have I seen this more than in working through my pain.

Years ago, I was really struggling with a deep hurt that was eating me up. The damage was showing up in every area of my life. As God began to restore my relationship with Him, I felt like God was urging me to offer forgiveness to the person who had been the source of my pain. Eventually, I was able to express it in a letter like this:

> *"I know that the healing I have experienced is from God for He is the one who initiates forgiveness by Christ's death and He is the one who can "restore the years the locusts have eaten." It is only because of God's forgiveness of me, that I am able to even forgive you. My faith is in a strong and loving God. I know He will continue to heal me from the effects of your wrong actions. He is my redeemer and the one who makes me whole. He has restored my soul. Regardless of how you respond to all of this, God has shown me the pathway of forgiveness and it has led me straight to the foot of the cross, where I have found comfort in the arms of a loving God and balm to heal the wounds of my broken heart."*

It's is interesting to reread this now, after so many years, and reflect on what God has done since then. Even back then, when I was just beginning this journey of rediscovering the gospel, the source of my healing was anchored in who God is and what He has done for me. As the gospel of grace seeps into our hearts not only does it restore our relationship with God but it offers us the hope of restored relationships with others and a path through our pain.

DEFINED BY
☐PAIN ☐PAST
☐CIRCUMSTANCES

i was...   i am...

rejected   bitter
abused   lonely
controlled   Controlling
judged   afraid
hurt   angry

SEPARATION

Orphan

LIVING AS AN ORPHAN

Unfortunately, in this life I will never fully live in the reality of who I am as His child. All of us fall short of full repentance and resting in the gospel. And there are times when, even though I crave it, I will refuse grace. I will reject the cross and convince myself that my resources for managing my sin are adequate and that my idolatry is really not that big of a deal. Quickly my life becomes a shadow of what it was meant to be as I live out of self-reliance rather than God-reliance.

Reading the book *From Fear to Freedom* by Rose Marie Miller opened my eyes to how I was living as a spiritual orphan. I picked it up at a conference we went to where Jack and Rose Marie were speaking on the Fatherhood of God. I couldn't really follow all that they were saying—because I had not really tasted grace or grasped the fullness of the gospel. But on the way out the door I bought her book. Later that night, as I read through the pages, I felt like I was not only reading my own story but I was getting a spiritual diagnosis of my heart. *Finally,* I had an explanation for my daily reality!

Close your eyes for a minute and picture an orphan. You might imagine an abandoned child on the streets of New York City, a starving child roaming the streets of Calcutta, or a toddler trapped in a cage in an orphanage in Guatemala. Let your senses make this picture come alive. Imagine not only the sounds and smells, but how that child would develop emotionally and spiritually if she is never rescued.

Now imagine that child being adopted, but refusing to sleep in a bed. Or leaving the dinner table to go and look for food in the streets. Or chaining herself to her bed in order to feel safe.

Hard to imagine, I know. But spiritually, *this is us.* We go on living as orphans even though we have *already* been adopted and brought into a family.

After hearing how the gospel transformed Rose Marie from living like an orphan to living like a daughter, I had a much clearer picture of what that might look like in my own life, but I needed a chart to help me really get it. Consider this chart like an x-ray to expose the ways you might be living like a spiritual orphan.

	Orphan	Child
Description	Fearful, independent, untrusting, hopeless, insecure, self-reliant, trapped	Hopeful, dependant, trusting, joyful, secure, confident, content
Actions	Gossiping, blame-shifting, critical spirit, Bitter, debt collector, complaining, defensive, control freak, rebellious	Grace-giver, non-judgemental, accepts responsibility for self, forgives, prayerful, accepting, faith
View of God	Absentee father, condemning, score-keeping, judging, tolerates me, God is a taker	Father, care-taker, trustworthy, forgiving, deliverer, provider, sovereign, loving, faithful, God is giver
View of Sin	Pharisee/moralist, deceives self, someone who sometimes sins, external focus on actions	I'm worse than I think, understands self-effort as a lack of faith, focus on attitudes of the heart
View of Self	Guilt-laden, self-reliant, moral will power, what do others think, trapped by circumstances, unworthy, fixer-upper	Sinner, dependant, free, forgiven, saint, loved
View of Grace	Earn God's favor, Christ is not enough, not worthy to receive, not necessary for daily tasks, an aid to your own effort	Needed for both salvation and growth, daily dependance

Note: For additional copies of this chart, visit www.CravingGrace.org.

The descriptions here are really just the symptoms of an identity crisis. When we live as orphans, we are rejecting the identity we have been given in Christ and are creating our own: one that is defined by our past, our pain, and our circumstances.

Our Past: includes our family situation (current family and family of origin), our accomplishments, what others have done to us, or what we have done to others (both good and bad).

Our Pain: encompasses how we have been hurt by others, by our circumstances, and by our own choices.

Our Circumstances: includes the season of life I am in (single, married, fertile, infertile, widowed, divorced, stay-at-home mom, career mom, single parent, grandparent, empty nester, senior citizen) and my current life situation (going through a divorce, fighting cancer, rising to the top in my career, excelling as an athlete, starting a business, transitioning from working at home to working full time).

Here's the equation that shows the grip these three things might have in your own life:

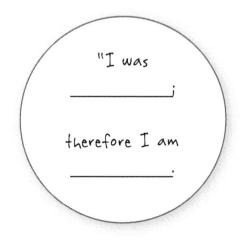

"I was

_____;

therefore I am

_____.

I WAS	THEREFORE I AM
Controlled	Bitter
Abused	Angry
Successful	Proud
Neglected	Independent
Misled	Anxious
Sick	Over-Protective
Criticized	Critical

If you're like me, reading that list probably made you cringe.

That's because I see myself in many of those descriptions. I allow myself to be consumed by the residual effects of my past, my pain, and my current situation. When my situation is going well, I'm confident and in control. When my situation becomes difficult or desperate, I quickly can become fearful, frustrated, and angry.

When I live as an orphan it is all up to me. I think that I succeed or fail based solely on my own self effort. I can remember a time, back when our children were young and I felt completely inadequate in my role as a wife and mother, which illustrates this orphan spirit perfectly.

Earlier in the day I had stripped the beds and put all the sheets in the washing machine. As we were putting the kids to bed that evening I realized that there were no sheets on the beds and quickly ran out to the garage to switch the load.

This is no big deal, right? Put other sheets on the bed let the kids stay up later, or just camp out in the living room on sleeping bags.

Well, I must have been out in the garage for quite awhile because David came out looking for me to see if everything was okay. I cannot imagine how he must have felt when he saw me sitting on the garage floor, knees curled to my chest, leaning against the washing machine, bawling. I'm sure he heard me muttering, "I am such a failure. What kind of mother can't keep clean sheets on the bed? What kind of loser can't remember to change the laundry? I don't deserve to be a wife OR a mother!" Of course he gently reassured me that it really was no big deal and I finally went inside.

Remembering that story brings all those emotions right back to the center of my chest. Obviously, I had reached the end of my rope. In my case, living like an orphan means that I feel great when I get it right, and am miserable when I don't. I transfer this same reality to my relationship with God.

On days when I perform well, I pat myself on the back and grab my Pharisee hat and parade around. On days when I fail miserably, I put on sackcloth and ashes and beat myself up. Both results are completely dependent on my performance. It's all about me.

As a spiritual orphan I might serve and minister to others, but I'll do it out of a sense of duty rather than devotion. I may remember that I'm justified by faith and the grace of Christ, but I'm pretty sure my sanctification is based on my self-effort. And so what God meant for blessing—living a life of dependence on Him, based on a heart of faith and worship—becomes a terrible curse, living on a treadmill of performance and disappointment.

There are two reasons why you might be living like an orphan. You might be a believer in Jesus, but find yourself living more like an orphan than a child. This doesn't mean that you are not a Christian—*it just means that you are missing out on the most amazing blessings of our Salvation.* You are not experiencing life as God intended it to be lived, as an adopted child enjoying the benefits of life in God's family. This is why we need to remember the gospel, preach it to ourselves, repent, and run to the cross. **It's easy to forget what Christ has done, to think it's all about me, and to do it my way. The gospel compels us to think differently.**

Or, you might be living as a spiritual orphan—*because you really are.* If you have never admitted your need for God, confessed your sinner's heart, and believed in what Christ did on the cross, then you are a spiritual orphan. You are living outside God's family spinning around in the pit of orphan despair. But the answer for you is the same—remember the gospel, repent of your sin, ask Christ to forgive you, and run to the cross. You'll be restored and given a new identity as God's child.

DIGGING DEEPER

Living as His Child vs. Living Like an Orphan

1. List as many people you can think of from the Old and New Testaments whose identity was changed by their encounter with the living God.

2. Read Psalm 145. As you read, make a list of all the descriptions of God. As you look at each description on your list, see how who He is connects to your identity. He is _____; I am _____.

3. In the Gospel Eight diagram, the interior of the top circle reflects our identity in Christ. As you think about all the characteristics of God that can be squeezed in there, which ones are you the most thankful for?

4. Which of the following do you tend to gain most of your identity from: Your past, your pain, or your circumstances?

5. Look at the chart on page 59 comparing life as an orphan and life as a child. Circle all the adjectives that best describe you. This is a good reality check, but may be a bit sobering. Afterwards the typical response to this exercise is, "How do I move from living like an orphan to living like a daughter?" Based on what you have been learning, how would you answer that?

6. How would you recreate the "I was _____; I am _____" chart to reflect your own past and how it affects you in the present?

I WAS	THEREFORE I AM

7. Read Ezekiel 16, an allegory about unfaithful Jerusalem. Although graphic, it is a perfect picture that shows how God rescues us as orphans, and makes a covenant with us, His children.

8. What is your own story of *loss* and *restoration*?

A CHILD RESPONDS TO SIN

As a Christian, I'm still going to be confronted by my sin and unbelief. The beauty of the gospel is that the answer is simple for someone who knows they are God's child—run to the cross. "In repentance and rest is your salvation; in quietness and trust is your strength" (Isaiah 30:15).

The cross is strong enough to bear the weight of all of my inadequacies, my fears, my pain, my sorrow, and my grief. One of my favorite phrases in the Old Testament is "He remembers that we are dust" (Psalm 103:14). This is such great comfort. He knows me, He gets me, and He knows that my faith is faltering. I believe, yet I don't believe. **God knows exactly what to do with my unbelief.**

In Mark 9, as Jesus, James, and John return from the transfiguration, a man has brought his sick child to the disciples for healing, only to find that they can't heal him. When Jesus hears this, he exclaims: "Oh, unbelieving generation…bring the boy to me." The father explains the son's illness and says, "…if you can do anything, take pity on us and help us."

Jesus can't believe the question. "'If I can?' Of course I can! Anything is possible for him who believes." To that, the father exclaimed. **"I do believe; help me overcome my unbelief!"** Then Jesus healed his son.

I **love** this! *He remembers that we are dust.* There are many days when I repeat it over and over in my head: "Lord, I believe, help me in my unbelief!" The beautiful thing about this is it's true! It is safe to confess our unbelief because He will not lash out at us. Remember, His wrath is finished!

There is a sweet group of moms that meet once a week at my son's school. We pray for the students and teachers, but we also pray for each other. Today one of these dear women broke down and cried while she prayed, confessing her anger at the painful circumstances they are facing as a family, but also confessing her unbelief. As tears were streaming down her face, she prayed, "I am going to keep saying 'I trust you, Lord,' until I start to believe it."

So even with wavering faith, I can confess my unbelief and run to the cross, resting in my Father's love and what Christ has done for me.

A few verses later in Isaiah 30:18 we get a beautiful picture of God's longing for us, even though we may resist Him. "Yet the Lord longs to be gracious to you; he rises to show you compassion."

It is so easy to get discouraged by our sin and the unbelief that wreaks havoc in our hearts, but if we really understand our identity in Christ we will realize that there are two things that are true about me—**all the time**.

- Because I am forgiven and clothed in the righteousness of Christ, I am seen as a saint in His eyes.

- Because I am a sinner, corrupted by a sinful nature, I will continue to sin.

So the dual reality is that I am both a **Saint** and a **Sinner**. They are equally true all the time. One does not negate the other. If we only grasp the part that we are sinner, then we will be characterized by self-loathing and moaning and groaning about our unworthiness. The focus is on us and not on Christ. It minimizes what Christ has done. On the other hand, if we focus only on the fact that we are saints, then we tend to minimize our sin, which makes a mockery of His death. Seeing myself as **both** a Saint and a Sinner reminds me that **I am desperately in need of His grace—it is what saves me and it is what propels me forward in my growth as a Christian.**

AN ORPHAN
RESPONDS TO SIN

When living like an orphan, I will at times look deep into the mirror and feel the stirring of the Spirit prompting me to repent and believe.

As easy as it sounds to turn and trust the gospel—it's not always so easy to do. Remember the whole, "but you would have none of it" phrase from Isaiah 30:15. So often I choose to bypass the cross, striving to find my own way out of the pit.

Ironically, this self-effort simply drives me deeper into a life of self-reliance that takes me further away from God.

I reject the simple way of the gospel (repent and believe) and choose a harder path—a path that requires me to summon my energy, work hard to gain the approval of others and God, and either bury or nurse my pain. Here I go, circling around and around and around.

This is what happens when we make repentance primarily about fixing our behavior and "getting better." We start with the fruit instead of the root: try harder, do more, pray more, have a quiet time, do this list of ten things that lead to holiness, and on and on.

It's not that our actions are unimportant; it's that our actions can't be the first thing we focus on. Otherwise, we end up like the Israelites.

> "…the Gentiles, who did not pursue righteousness, have obtained it, a righteousness that is by faith; but Israel, who pursued a law of righteousness, has not attained it. Why not? **Because they pursued it not by faith but as if it were by works.** They stumbled over the 'stumbling stone'" (Romans 9:30-32).

They stumbled over Christ, because they couldn't accept that their righteousness was not based on their *own effort.*

> "Are you so foolish? After beginning with the Spirit, **are you now trying to attain your goal by human effort?**…Does God give you his Spirit and work miracles among you because you observe the law, or because you **believe what you heard?**" (Galatians 3:3-5).

In the reflection questions at the end of the last section I asked you to consider how we move from living as an orphan to living as a child. The answer is by FAITH—**believe what you heard.**

It is as easy and as hard as the challenge of Jesus—to repent and believe. Repent and believe.

What types of things do I need to believe to see this change take place?

I need to remember and believe the truth about:

- Who Christ is
- What He has done for me
- Who God is
- All the spiritual blessings I have in Christ
- God's Word
- That God is in control
- That He loves me
- That He knows me
- That He sees me
- That He delights in me
- And on and on and on

One day, years ago I was really struggling and called my friend, Tricia, and unloaded on her. She realized it was a bit much to tackle over the phone so she invited me over for lunch. As we sat and talked she made a statement that has stuck with me and become a part of my spiritual DNA. She said, **"The truth can transform you as much as a lie can destroy you."** Simple, but profound.

The statement launched a whole new journey in my heart to help me uncover the lies that I believed and how they were strangling me. No matter what emotional hole you are sitting in, you probably got there by believing lies. God can rescue you from the pit when you turn your eyes and heart back to Him.

Believing the truth is a fight. Your mind and heart conjure up so many lies about God, yourself, your pain, and your circumstances. Satan is the father of lies and he wants you to be suspicious of God's love and plans for you. When living in the vortex of life as an orphan, it will be a battle to tell yourself the truth when the lies are screaming louder. Even as I write this, I am battling the lies and voices in my head. Honestly, sometimes it feels like I am back in middle school. "Who do you think you are? What do you have to say that hasn't already been said? God only uses people who have their act together. If these readers knew what a mess you are they wouldn't even read this. Blah, Blah, Blah." **Only truth can silence the lies.**

In Rose Marie's book *From Fear to Freedom*, she uses an illustration to describe our desperation. When we are stuck living as an orphan we are like a caterpillar that is encircled by a raging inferno. There's no way that a caterpillar can escape a ring of fire. Deliverance can only come if a hand reaches down and pulls it out of the fire. *Deliverance comes from above.*

> "I waited patiently for the LORD; he turned to me and heard my cry. He lifted me out of the slimy pit, out of the mud and mire; he set my feet on a rock and gave me a firm place to stand. He put a new song in my mouth, a hymn of praise to our God. Many will see and fear and put their trust in the LORD." (Psalm 40:1-3).

For us, being rescued out of our orphan pit is both as **easy** and as **hard** as *remembering the gospel*. On one hand, it's simple and easy to just admit my sin, ask God to forgive me, then enjoy a restored relationship with Him. On the other hand, fighting the lies, swallowing my pride, admitting my need, confessing my sin, letting go of my pain—these can be the hardest things ever!

Most of the time I can't even tell when I am living like an orphan. I am so blind. A few months ago, David and I were having one of those "discussions" that was not getting resolved. It was making me grumpy, irritable, and angry. My friend, Valerie and I exercise together a few times a week, and so she had been listening to me process it all for a few days. Finally, one day as I am putting my bike up into the garage and closing the door she calls out to me, "Ruthie, you know you are living like an orphan, right?" So, I reached up and pushed the button to close the garage door. As I did, she jumped in the path of the detectors to stop the door from closing and boldly proclaimed, "And I'm not going anywhere until you admit it."

That my friends, is good stuff! When we can't see it ourselves, usually our friends can. God puts them in our lives to help us remember the gospel and drive us back to Him.

DIGGING DEEPER

Our Response to Sin

1. When you respond to your sin and repent, how do you view God's response? Is it filled with love, forgiveness, contempt, or disapproval? Read Luke 15 which captures three stories of repentance. In each one, what is the response to repentance?

2. Based on this passage, how does your picture of God need to be adjusted to align with Scripture?

3. Why do you choose to manage your sin through false repentance, versus running to the cross for complete healing and grace? What is it that drives you to resist His grace rather than run to it?

4. What are the voices you hear in your head when you know you have failed or when you are afraid to fail? The messages you hear in those moments are a clue to the lies that you believe. (Remember my story about the sheets in the previous section? What was I telling myself? What was I *really* believing?)

5. When you reflect on the pain of your past and the bitter fruit that it has produced in your life (see question #6 from page 65), can you identify any vows that you may have made that reinforce the lies that you believe or are susceptible to? Examples might be, "I will never let

anyone see me cry," or "I can't count on anyone else but myself." You may want to keep a record of these messages as the Lord reveals them; you must know what these lies are if you want to sever their roots and believe the truth.

REST OR RESIST

You are probably familiar with the verse "Be still and know that I am God" (Psalm 46:10). It is a sweet invitation from a loving Father for us to rest, listen, and wait on Him. Yet I hate this verse. I don't do "still" very well and I certainly don't do "rest" very well.

The intersection of the diagram, where the two circles come together, asks the question, "Will I rest in or resist the gospel?" This reminds me of a railroad crossing sign, and as I battle my unbelief I can hear those warning bells a ringin'!

What happens at the intersection? Here's the short answer: *when the Spirit works in our hearts to show us our sin and point us to Christ, we can either run to the cross and rest in our Father's love and forgiveness, or we can resist the cross and make our own way, relying on our self-sufficiency and cheap substitutes for a Savior.*

Now, if you're like me, a longer answer will probably be a little more helpful.

What does it look like to rest—a *rest* that leads to *rest*oration?

I know in my life, the reason I don't rest in His love for me is that I am suspicious of His love. Letting Him love me and be in control of things puts me in a vulnerable place. I feel more secure when I am in control and micromanaging my world, than when He is. *Do you hear the irony in that?* It reminds me of the can of pineapples in Kelly's story. "No God, I'm good. I got this."

So what would it take to move me from **resisting** to **resting**? We're back to repentance and faith: repenting of the lies I am believing that keep me from resting in Him and *replacing those lies with the truth.*

I know that each of us struggle with a different set of lies. But in my life these are the ones that sink me:

- He isn't in control
- He doesn't know me
- He has abandoned me
- He doesn't act for my good (my definition of good)
- He doesn't love me

In essence, we have exchanged what is true about God for a lie. It is these lies that keep us from resting in Him.

When I was a little girl we lived overseas and I always looked forward to someone sending us the JC Penny catalog. My favorite section was the bedrooms. You know those rooms with the matching curtains, rugs, wallpaper, and comforter in a print similar to one you would find on the outside of a box of tissue?

My eyes were always drawn to the canopy beds. I dreamed of sleeping under a canopy bed. It didn't help that we lived in Europe and every castle and palace I visited had amazing canopy beds!

Since a canopy bed is so inviting, let's use that as an illustration to help us understand what it means to rest in the Father's love. With four posts, we'll let each post represent a truth we need to believe about God in order to move from resisting to resting. Listed below is each truth and a few related verses that will help you understand each one.

1. **God is in Control:** Acts 17:26, Psalm 139: 14-16, Philippians 2:12-13, Psalm 115:3, and Psalm 33

2. **God knows Me:** Genesis 16, Psalm 103:14, Psalm 139, and Isaiah 49:15-17

3. **God will never leave me:** Joshua 1:5, Deuteronomy 31:8, Hebrews 13:5-7, John 14:18-27, and 2 Corinthians 1:3-5

4. **God acts for my Good and for His Glory:** Philippians 2:12-14, Romans 8:28-29, 1 Peter 1:7, Ephesians 1:11-12, Jeremiah 29:11, and Isaiah 55:9 (His definition of good!)

These truths alone aren't enough to make me want to fall back on that bed and rest. Unless I become absolutely convinced that He loves me, then it's not worth the risk.

So the fifth truth that **God Loves Me** is like the canopy covering that four poster bed. I would say this is the most important truth of all—it makes the others come alive.

It reminds me of the song, *His Banner over Me is Love*, that I used to sing when I was a little girl, and the verses from Zephaniah 3:17 where it says, "He will take great delight in you, he will quiet you with his love, he will rejoice over you with singing."

It's this kind of love that gives me the security to take the plunge into that big canopy bed and rest!

But for many of us letting God love us is difficult, even painful. **We don't trust Him to be good with His love.** The pain of our past keeps us from allowing God, or anyone, to love us.

Yet my ability to rest in Him is directly tied to who He is. **Do I believe it or not? Am I willing to trust Him? Am I willing to let him love me? Am I willing to believe that He can heal and redeem the broken pieces of my heart? Am I willing to trust that He will be good with His love?**

These five truths are based on who God is: His identity and His character. They can all be written in the top portion of the circle (along with about a zillion other truths about God!). Go back and reread those five truths.

If I asked you if you believed them, you would likely say yes. Not so fast. It's hard work to uncover what we *really* believe about God, mainly because most of us have spent many years suppressing what we really think and feel about

Him. We feel anger, betrayal, and jealousy; yet we don't see how often these are rooted in a lie we are holding onto about God. Many years ago, in preparing for a talk, I collected a series of candid statements from friends. Here are just a few:

- *I desperately cry out for friends who really know me and love me and You leave me alone and disconnected. You don't want what's best for me.*

- *God why You are willing to sit back and allow "our" daughter to ruin her life with all these bad choices. Why are You not doing anything?! Are You really the "Father to the fatherless?"*

- *Father, why have You delayed or denied a husband for me? Am I too broken, too ugly or have my sins been so great that I blew it?*

- *"You've blessed all these other women with children but not me. You don't care about me or my desires."*

- *"I still feel guilty after all this time. You didn't forgive me."*

- *I prayed for You to heal my mother. You didn't. She died. You are not a healer.*

- *My husband has a pornography addiction. You are not powerful enough to break this cycle and save our marriage.*

- *My husband left me for another woman. You could have stopped him but You didn't. Where were You?*

- *Every day for a year, I've begun my day fearful that I am a bad mother. You can't give me victory over my anxiety.*

- *My cousin molested me throughout my childhood. You saw it all and didn't intervene. You must not be able to protect Your children from harm.*

- *You asked me to share my heart with my LIFE group. All I got was the blank stares. You set me up for rejection.*

- *My 13-year-old daughter doesn't have a single Christian friend to encourage and support her, despite many efforts from us both. You've thrown her to the wolves!*

- *It takes all the strength that I have to get out of bed every day. You promised me "an abundant life," but all I have is depression. You lied.*

Wow. Those are painfully honest confessions. Can we be that honest? Are you able to express how you really feel about God and your circumstances?

By reading these statements do you see how our perspective on our circumstances can expose what we really believe about God?

This is so important because eventually what we believe about God will show up in how we live our lives, walk through our pain, and make choices about the future.

I don't really care what you **say** you believe about God. I care what you **really** believe about God. If the lies seem hidden from you right now, stop and ask God to begin a process of peeling back the layers and showing you what's really there.

You cannot begin the process of replacing the lie with truth, until you first know what lie you are believing. I love the moment of clarity in the passage from Isaiah 44 that we looked at earlier. "Is not this thing that I hold in my right hand a lie?"

It's amazing how often we hold onto our lies with a fierce, white-knuckled grip. There is a woman in the Old Testament who understands exactly what we are up against in this fight for faith.

The Widow of Zarephath just might be one of my favorite ladies in the Bible. We find her story in 1 Kings 17. I hope you will take time to read it later. Here is a woman in great pain. She is a widow raising her son in a land shriveled up by drought. She is at the end of herself, her hope, and her food. In fact, she is collecting wood to cook her last meal. If there was ever a woman stuck like a caterpillar in a ring of fire, she is it!

Along comes Elijah, prophet of God, who has been stuck in a dried up ravine being fed by ravens. (I am sure he smelled lovely!) He sees her gathering wood and asks her to make him a cake.

I wish this were on YouTube. I would love to see the expression on her face or find out if she whacked him over the head with a stick. *Are you serious?* She has enough oil and flour for one more loaf of bread, and Elijah wants cake?

He promises her that if she makes him a cake that she will have enough oil and flour, and that it won't run dry—ever.

For a woman in survival mode this is the ultimate test! Will she listen? Trust? Or walk away?

We are just like her. We are desperately clinging to our oil and flour believing that what we **can see** is safer than what we **can't see**.

The Widow of Z is a courageous woman. I want to be just like her when I grow up. **She baked him a cake!** And another, and another, and another. The oil and flour did not run dry. There was always enough.

She is rescued and boldly proclaims in verse 24, **"Now I know who you are and that what you say is truth."** I love the irony here. She is not even a Jew and she is making a confession that the people of Israel had failed to make because they turned their backs on God and went their own way.

She trusted and was not disappointed. She opened the door for God to do a NEW thing in her heart. But it doesn't stop there. The end of the chapter records the account of her son getting sick and dying. This does not go over well, and in her anger she lashes out at Elijah and His God. Even though they are the object of her wrath, her son is miraculously healed. By setting aside what she was clinging to (her oil and flour) and putting her trust and hope in a promise, she experienced the blessing of faith and repentance.

That's my prayer for all of us: that we can set aside what we are clinging to and say with her, **"Now I know who you are and what you say is truth."**

Then, and only then, can we fall back into that big canopy bed, and rest. *Whoosh!*

Rest or Resist

1.   Of the 5 truths in this section which is the hardest for you to believe and why?

     • **God is in control.**
     • **God knows Me.**
     • **God will never leave me.**
     • **God acts for my good and for His glory.**
     • **He loves me.**

2.   Why is *really* believing God loves you essential to resting in Him?

3.   The grid on the following page can be helpful in discovering the lies that you are clinging to. Begin by writing **one** of the 5 truths about God, then answer the questions in each column. As you work through this it will reveal what you really believe about God and how it is impacting your life.

4.   Read 1 Kings 17 and review the story of the Widow of Z. How does her courage impact you? What would you have done if you were in her shoes?

God says He is _____	
I don't believe this truth because...	
When I don't believe this truth...	**If I really believed this truth...**
how do I relate to others?	how would I relate to others?
how do I view my circumstances?	how would I view my circumstances?
how do I view myself?	how would I view myself?
how do I relate to God?	how would I relate to God?
what Idol do I run to?	what would repentance look like?

Note: For additional copies of this chart, visit www.CravingGrace.org.

THE CYCLE IN
REAL LIFE

You've probably noticed by now that this diagram is drawn as a fluid figure eight.

Sanctification is a process. It's a process of becoming more like Christ—a process of recognizing *how great my sin is, how big the cross is, and how much I need* Jesus. It's a process of expanding my view of the greatness of God, becoming more dependent on Him and less self-reliant. It is a process of learning that my life is about making much of Jesus, and not much of me.

I didn't always believe this. In fact when I was 21 if you had asked me to describe a "godly woman," I would have described an old lady with blue-grey hair that had "gotten it together" to the point that she rarely needed Jesus. Now, I may not have said it aloud. But I can *guarantee* you that is what I really thought deep inside. And I was on a mission to get there—before you! The glorious reality is that I am not going to "get better" unless my definition of "getting better" is needing Jesus more. As I see just how deep the rabbit hole goes, I will see more and more how desperately I need a Savior.

A humorous way for me to see how the grace has captured my heart is to take a look back and remember what I would consider to be my "theme songs" growing up. If you had been around me during some key stages of my life, what would you have heard me singing?

As a pre-teen with a hairbrush "microphone" behind closed doors, you would have heard me belting Helen Reddy's, *I am Woman, Hear Me Roar*. As a senior in high school reeling from a series of destructive relationships, you would have heard me singing *Ain't Nothing Gonna Break My Stride, Ain't Nothing Gonna Slow Me Down* by Matthew Wilder. As a mother of three young children surrounded by toys and chaos, you would have heard me singing *I Will Survive* by Gloria Gaynor. Now, as a middle aged woman within a stone's throw of the empty nest (and menopause right around the corner), I am humming the phrases of an old hymn: *I need thee, Oh, I need thee, every hour I need thee.* In fact I sang it today as my college-aged kids were driving back to school. Trust me, I am painfully aware of my failures and my need for His saving and sustaining grace.

The purpose of the diagram being fluid is to emphasize the point that we are all in process. That means that some days, when my faith is weak and I get sucked into believing the lies, my life will reflect a Gospel Eight where the bottom circle is *much* larger than the top circle. I'm living more as an orphan than a child.

On other days, when my heart is tender and I run to the cross, I will live more out of my identity in Christ so the top circle will be *much* larger than the bottom circle.

How I wish I could just erase the bottom portion of this figure eight and never have to deal with that pit!

But the Scriptures show that on this side of heaven the reality of the bottom circle will always be there. As we grow in our faith and His grace sanctifies us, it will grow smaller, reflecting His work in our hearts. Until the world is made new and we are united with Christ, our sin and rebellion will be a constant reminder of our need for a Savior.

The diagram is also fluid in another way as well. Imagine the diagram animated with motion going in the direction of the arrows. *What propels us forward? What drives you to the cross? What restores your relationship with God? What exposes your unbelief? What pursues you when you choose to go your own way? What rescues you when you are living in that pit?* **GRACE.**

In the beginning of this book I shared the story of my spiritual unraveling. There was a huge disconnect in my heart between what I knew in my head and the reality that I was living. I understood A LOT about the gospel, but I was missing one huge important piece: Grace. I didn't get it. In a lot of ways I still don't get it. But I know I need it—desperately.

Grace is the heartbeat of the gospel. It's what propels us forward and breathes life and healing into our hearts.

It's funny how God works. I woke up today to work on this section and a friend posted a song on her Facebook page that I had never heard before. It was *Grace Flows Down* by Christy Knockles. It describes Christ's death on the cross by saying, "grace flows down and covers me." That's true. Grace flows down, *but it also flows around*. It is always pushing me, no matter where I am, back to Jesus.

Child of God

DEFINED BY

Restoration

He is... **i am...**

KING

forgiver
redeemer
healer
Savior
deliverer
provider
defender
lover ♡

forgiven
redeemed
healed
saved
delivered
provided for
defended
loved ♡

Rest in the Gospel

Will I ? Resist

SWIMMING IN THE GOSPEL

After a friend of mine realized she had a small view of God and wasn't that excited about her faith, she asked what she could do to expand her view of God. Great question!

I like to think of it as "swimming in the gospel." Gospel truths are all around us—we just need to open our eyes. I encouraged her to begin by writing down anything that caused her to think differently about God or any experience that helped her see God in a new way. This was important because her "impression" of God was not based on how He revealed Himself in Scripture, but was an image of Him created by her own personal pain and story.

Glimpses of grace are all around us. You might be reminded of the gospel by a book you read, a movie you watch, a spectacular sunset, a view from a mountaintop, or even a country song! Echoes of redemption are everywhere, but the primary source for the truth about God will be found in His Word.

As God began doing a new work in me, every time I read a passage of Scripture that spoke to idolatry, I put an "I" beside it. I wrote a "J" beside verses about justification and an "A" beside passages about adoption. This step alone caused my senses to wake up and pay attention to what I was learning about the gospel.

I began listening differently in church to the songs that we sang, clinging to phrases that pointed me to the gospel. And as the Gospel Eight diagram unfolded in my head I could see the pattern reflected in passages of Scripture like Psalm 40.

Friends are also an important part of this process. It's important to have friends in your life who will remind you of the gospel and point you back to the cross when you are believing lies. Sometimes your friends will have to fight for your faith when you feel you have none.

A friend was going through a terrible crisis in her marriage, and as she emerged on the other side of her pain she told a group of us that we were like columns that surrounded her during her darkest days, but we were columns covered with pillows that she could lean into when she was too weak to stand. You don't need to walk this journey alone; ask others to walk with you as you fight for faith.

What are you swimming in? Do you feel like you are drowning in your faith, isolated and numb? Immerse yourself in the beauty of the gospel, and you will say, as the writer of Hebrews declared, "It is good for our hearts to be strengthened by grace" (Hebrews 13:9).

THE PURPOSE OF OUR ADOPTION

One thing that all of us have in common after the Fall is that we tend to look at everything in terms of how it affects us. It's easy to think it's all about me, all the time. As a culture we are **absorbed** with ourselves, our children, our work, and our families. But we misunderstand the gospel and the purpose of our salvation if we think it's all about us. We get to enjoy the benefits and blessings of it, but it is definitely not about us!

There's a phrase that rings out over and over again in the Old Testament. It is not always said the same way, but the theme remains...

"Then they will know that I am the Lord...."

That pretty much sums it up. The purpose of our salvation and adoption is for us to point others to Christ. John Piper reminds us to "make much of Jesus." Steve Brown encourages us to "smell like Jesus." The bottom line is that we are to live in such a way that God is glorified, we are satisfied, and others are drawn to Him.

Philippians 2:15 encourages us to shine like stars in the universe. Ephesians 1:12-14 describes it like this:

> *In order that we, who were the first to hope in Christ, might* **be for the praise of his glory.** *And you also were included in Christ when you heard the word of truth, the gospel of your salvation. Having believed you were marked in him with a seal, the promised Holy Spirit, who is a deposit guaranteeing our inheritance until the redemption of those who are God's possession*—**to the praise of his glory.**

As our hearts are enlarged by faith, the true miracle of our salvation and the blessing of our adoption, we can't help but respond. **We respond through renewed worship, renewed service and renewed joy—all for the praise of His glory, not ours.**

One day as I was explaining the Gospel Eight diagram, a woman remarked that she definitely was spinning around in the cycle of living like an orphan, even though she was a believer. She confessed, "Why would I want to invite anyone to join me? I don't want anyone to have to live like this."

What a great insight! It begs the question, "What are you inviting others into?" If you have a small view of God and live like an orphan, there really is not a lot to get excited about, is there? But if in living like a child, God has captured your heart, and you are undone by His holiness and humbled by His grace—that is something to celebrate and worthy of inviting others to join.

Can I just tell you that my favorite part of this diagram is the person holding the balloons with outstretched arms? It's an image that speaks volumes to me: Freedom. Joy. Peace. It's the picture of a person living with a heart full of faith. And it is an *invitation*—to you and to others. Join the party!

There is a decorative tile that sits in my kitchen window. It was given to me by a dear friend before she moved to South Africa. It simply says, "The Lord has done great things for us. Our hearts are filled with Joy" (Psalm 126:3). It reminds me that I have tasted and I have seen. I have tasted His grace and seen it work its way into my heart. He has changed me. Grace continues to drip its way into the parched places of my heart and bring healing.

You probably know what it's like when you are on the hunt for "just a little something sweet." You are looking for something that will hit the spot and satisfy your craving. A pack of Smarties might be good enough for some people, but that doesn't quite cut it with me. I am on the hunt for chocolate. I don't need a whole bag. *I just need a taste.*

Seems like a silly way to think about grace, but I cannot tell you how many times just a taste of His grace in any given situation has been enough to settle my heart and refocus my mind.

> "O, taste and see that the Lord is good. Blessed is the
> man who takes refuge in Him" (Psalm 34:8).

Take refuge in His love. Soak in the gospel—even if it is a slow drip. Let His grace saturate you, and then share it with those around you.

They are craving it, but they might not know it. Yet.

DIGGING DEEPER

The Cycle, Swim Lessons and Our Purpose

1. Take a moment and in the margin draw a Gospel 8 outline that is an honest reflection of where you are right now in your relationship with God. Which circle is larger and why?

2. What have been your theme songs during various stages of your life?

3. What does God use to awaken you to the beauty of the gospel?

4. Take a step back and honestly evaluate what you are currently swimming in. *What you 'swim in' is a reflection of what you are craving.*

5. Is there an adjustment that needs to be made in your life that would put you on a path to encounter more of a taste of His grace?

6. If by reading this you have discovered that you have a small view of God, your sin or the gospel, try keeping a list of the glimpses of grace that He brings into your life each day.

7. Ask God to give you a picture of how He can use you in your current situation to make His name great and invite others into relationship with Him.

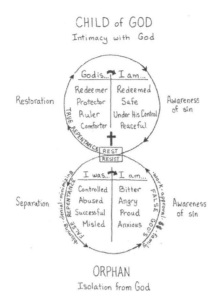

CHILD of GOD
Intimacy with God

God is... I am...

Redeemer | Redeemed
Protector | Safe
Ruler | Under His Control
Comforter | Peaceful

Restoration

TRUE REPENTANCE

Awareness
of sin

REST
RESIST

I was... I am...

Controlled | Bitter
Abused | Angry
Successful | Proud
Misled | Anxious

Separation

FALSE REPENTANCE
blame · denial · minimizing

work · approval/rules/... FALSE
G.O.D.

Awareness
of sin

ORPHAN
Isolation from God

DRAWING THE GOSPEL 8 DIAGRAM

Now that you understand the diagram, it's time for you to learn to draw it! I won't make you draw the tricky, detailed one. Instead I'll just ask you to draw the simple version I use when I teach. It's so easy that I have drawn it on the back of a receipt and on a napkin at a restaurant.

(Once you've seen this version you will be even more thankful that Deb took it and made it beautiful!)

It doesn't really matter how you draw this diagram, but, if you like step-by-step instructions, here is one suggestion of how it can be done.

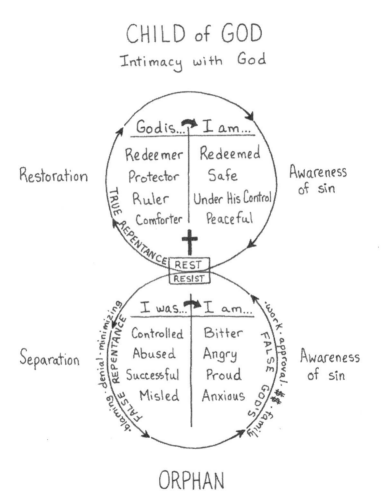

CHILD of GOD
Intimacy with God

Restoration

TRUE REPENTANCE

God is...   I am...

Redeemer   Redeemed
Protector   Safe
Ruler   Under His Control
Comforter   Peaceful

Awareness
of sin

REST
RESIST

Separation

FALSE REPENTANCE · denial · minimizing · blaming

I was...   I am...

Controlled   Bitter
Abused   Angry
Successful   Proud
Misled   Anxious

FALSE GOD'S · work · approval · $$ · family

Awareness
of sin

ORPHAN
Isolation from God

1.   Draw the figure eight and insert the directional arrows and cross.

2.   Label the outside of the top and bottom circles "Child" and "Orphan" as indicated.

3.   Label "Awareness of Sin," "Restoration," and "Separation."

4.   Label the bottom left curve with "False Repentance" on the inside curve and examples of the types on the outside curve.

5.   Label the bottom right curve with "False gods" inside the curve and examples of idolatry outside the curve.

6.   Label the interior of the top circle reflecting our identity in Christ. Note: You can list any attributes of God you choose. You do not have to use the ones I have chosen. You can also fill this circle with more than just the attributes of God and include all the riches of the gospel found throughout scripture.

7.   Label the interior of the bottom circle reflecting our identity as spiritual orphans. Note: There is no limit to what this list of descriptions can include. Choose the ones that relate best to your own story, or that you think will connect with who you are sharing this with. Make sure your list includes more than just 'negative' adjectives. We tend to think of descriptions like "competent" and "independent" as positive traits (which they can be) but when living as an orphan they are not. So be sure to include those as well.

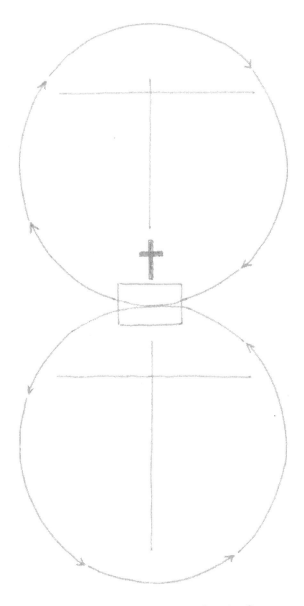

The only hard part about drawing this is remembering it! So make sure you practice it enough times that you can share it should God give you the opportunity. You can start with outline provided here. Also, remember to practice talking through it a few times out loud so that you can share it from your heart.

Not long after Deb learned about the Gospel 8, she had lunch with a friend who was battling breast cancer. As they talked, Deb realized that, for her friend, being diagnosed with cancer had been like a tsunami to her sense of identity. So Deb shared the diagram with her. A week later she read this on her friend's blog, *Pilgrims Pathway-Our Journey Together with Him,* in a section titled "One Thousand Gifts."

> **Gift #285** *Per dear Deb's doodle drawing lesson—I will choose to live as the greatly blessed child of God that I am, not a spiritual orphan. He is my forgiver: I confess my sin to Him and I am forgiven. He is my redeemer: I am redeemed by the blood of the Lamb. He is my Savior: I am saved through simple faith. He is my deliverer: I am delivered from every bondage to sin…delivered from eternal death/separation from Him, delivered from fear and doubt. He is my provider, and I am well provided for by Him in every way. He is my defender: I am defended. He is the lover of my soul: I am loved with an everlasting love. He is my healer, and I can trust Him to heal me if that is best. (Oh Lord, is it Your best to heal me of cancer, the invisible tourniquet sensation on my arm, the side effects/damage done from the*

chemo? I wish healing me would be Your very best! I pray so. Please help me to trust and rest in You and your will no matter what.) I know my absolute ultimate "perfect" healing will be a new body in Heaven, worshipping Him there forever, just not sure about the here and now on earth part. Because of my position in Christ, I do not have to "live as an orphan" or give in to bitterness, loneliness, a controlling nature, fear, doubt, blaming others, broken relationships, or anger OR ANY OTHER SUCH THING. God has MUCH better for me! Thank You Lord and Deb for the "doodle drawing lesson" spelling this out for me!

What a great picture of God's truth and grace seeping into the cracked places of a heart and bringing healing! All because Deb shared a bit of truth and grace with a hurting friend. *Don't be surprised* if God's put someone in your path that needs to hear the truth of God's grace embedded in this diagram. *Don't be afraid* to scribble it on whatever is handy. **Then be amazed when God does what only God can do!**

Child of God

DEFINED BY

Restoration

He is...   i am...

KING

forgiver   forgiven
redeemer   redeemed
healer   healed
Savior   saved
deliverer   delivered
provider   provided for
defender   defended
lover   loved

Rest in the Gospel

Will I   ?   Resist

STARTING A NEW LIFE

If reading this booklet and studying the diagram has prompted you to consider Jesus for the first time, I'd like to share what your next steps might be. Maybe you feel separated from God, like you are spinning around in the bottom circle with no one who really cares. There's hope. The solution in moving towards a relationship with God begins with taking a long look in the mirror, at the broken and messy places of your heart, then looking up at the cross.

Faith in Christ involves three things:

Admit that you are a sinner. Not just that you sin, but that your heart is tainted with sin which corrupts your entire being. Your sin is what separates you from God. He is holy and hates sin. That's why He had to punish his only Son. Someone had to pay for your sin.

Believe that outside of Christ there is no solution, no forgiveness, no lasting peace. **Believe** that Christ died for your sin and that not only can He wipe your slate clean with the cross, but that He'll also throw away the slate! He is not going to judge you for all the wrongs things you do. Instead He will give you the righteousness that Jesus earned by living a perfect life. When you trust Him to take away your sin, He sees you as clothed in the beauty and perfection of Christ.

Confess your need for a Savior and ask Him to forgive you. Trust in Christ to be your Deliverer and look to what Jesus has done for you on the cross. God will forgive you and restore you as His child.

This is the doorway of the gospel. If you have taken these steps, welcome to the family! You've begun a relationship with God. Ahead of you is a new journey of walking with God through ups and downs and twists and turns. But on the path is every promise, every truth about God, every spiritual blessing that is offered to His children! You have been given a new identity as His child, and you will forever be a part of His family. Nothing can separate you from the love of God.

As you begin this relationship with God you will want to surround yourself with people who can encourage you and equip you along the way. Find a community of believers where you can grow in your new faith. Enjoy the blessings of adoption and **REMEMBER** the gospel! **Even as you continue to sin and struggle with doubt and unbelief, remember that the solution is always the same: run to the cross. It changes everything!**

USING THIS BOOK
WITH A GROUP

There are a couple of ways you can use this book with a small group.

The standard way would be for each member to read a section ahead of time and be prepared to share their thoughts and discuss the *Digging Deeper* questions together.

An alternative would be to read the section together, either out loud or silently, when you meet. The sections are not that long and would only take a few minutes to read. The advantage of this method is that everyone is literally, 'on the same page' and prepared. Then you can move through a discussion and answer the *Digging Deeper* questions.

Some of you are teachers and will want to use this material as a springboard to leading your own study. It is pretty obvious that there is still much to be shared about each of the topics covered in this book. **Remember, it was only written to start the conversation!** So as a teacher you could easily expand on any of them and add your own stories, scriptures and illustrations.

You might want to study this book together while at the same time reading *From Fear to Freedom* by Rose Marie Miller or *The Transforming Power of the Gospel* by Jerry Bridges. (Or any other gospel-centered resource!)

The questions at the end of each section are simply meant as a guide for discussion. I provided more questions than you will likely be able to cover. As a leader you might want to select a few that seem appropriate for your group.

However you choose to pursue this, I pray it will be a blessing!

ADDITIONAL RESOURCES

The list below includes titles that have had an amazing impact on my journey in learning to believe and apply the gospel to my life. If you are looking to grow, then dive into these life-changing books.

- *Bold Love*, Dan Allender
- *Surrender to Love*, David G. Benner
- *Transforming Grace*, by Jerry Bridges
- *Trusting God Even When Life Hurts*, by Jerry Bridges
- *The Transforming Power of the Gospel*, by Jerry Bridges
- *Prodigal God*, Tim Keller
- *Counterfeit Gods*, Tim Keller
- *From Fear to Freedom*, Rose Marie Miller
- *Desiring God*, John Piper
- *Future Grace*, John Piper
- *Strong Women Soft Hearts*, Paula Rinehart
- *A Praying Life*, Paul E. Miller
- *Everyday Prayers*, Scotty Smith (devotional)
- *A Gospel Primer*, Milton Vincent (devotional)
- *Addictions: A Banquet in the Grave*, Edward T. Welch
- *Gospel Centered Life* (World Harvest Mission) Bible Study

I would also recommend Steve L. Childers' article, "True Spirituality: The Transforming Power of the Gospel."

BLOG POSTS FROM SARAH DELK

The following are excerpts of blog posts written by my daughter Sarah. I hope that including them here will give you an inside look at what it looks like to wrestle with the gospel and fight for faith. She has a unique gift of expressing what is going on in her heart, and I hope it will encourage you.

You can read more at delk-sarah.tumblr.com

I'm tired of being numb.

Preface: I'm using the term "Gospel" in this post to mean the good news about Jesus—simply that he died for my sinfulness to bring me into his family.

I'm tired of being numb to the Gospel. I have heard that I'm broken and Jesus died to save me from my brokenness so I could live forever with him so many times.

When any pastor/teacher/youth leader starts with the typical gospel illustration, I typically zone out and think about the fact that I "already know this stuff—I can't get anything out of it."

I am so foolish.

This is not an appropriate response to the Gospel. My youth intern once said that the Gospel should awe our hearts and move us to action EVERY time we hear it…and if it isn't, something isn't clicking.

I heard a pretty basic Gospel presentation at a Campus Crusade meeting last week at UF. I had to catch myself at the very beginning from zoning out...I stopped right there and asked God to give me ears to hear—even if I had "heard" it a million times. Because the reality is, the fact that God knows my heart and loves me anyway should bring me to my knees in confession and adoration.

And so often it doesn't.

I want to cherish the Gospel as if my life depended on it. Because quite frankly, it does. When I was justified once and for all, I was brought from death into life. So my life, my eternal life, depends on the Gospel.

But I'm learning more and more every day that believing the Gospel isn't just a one-time thing. It's an every-moment-of-every-day kind of thing. My life depends on the Gospel every day as I believe the truth about who God is and who I am. In return I am transformed and renewed.

THAT's why I need to hear it a million times. THAT's why I don't want to be numb to the Gospel...because I want to be transformed by it. I want to be compelled to action every time I hear it, absolutely in awe of God's love for me despite of my brokenness. I want my view of my sinfulness and my view of God's holiness to grow exponentially every time I hear about the sweetness of what was accomplished in the cross.

I want to cherish the Gospel as if my life depends on it. Because it does.

My Identity-My Plans.

This is such a consistent theme in my life. I'm not kidding you, my mind is constantly planning things. I make my plans in two ways.

A) By planning my days—when I will wake up, leave, work, sleep, relax, etc.

B) By planning what I have to get done.

So in the A example—I find my identity in my plans by planning my days. I want to know when everything is going to happen so I can figure my entire day out—minute by minute. The root of all of this is that I want to be in control. I want to manipulate my time in such a way that things work out exactly how I want them to. In the B example, planning what I have to get done, I tend to organize and over-analyze little details. I figure out how much I need to do, when I need to do it, and then work as hard as possibly can to get it all done as soon as humanly possible.

But wait, you might be asking—what's so wrong with organizing and getting things done? Nothing is wrong with those things. But it's been very easy for me to see when these plans become an idol in my life. *As soon as I start believing that getting things done is more important than spending time with Christ or investing in others*—that's when my plans become an idol. And unfortunately, it happens all the time.

The root of all of this, I realized recently, is that I crave peace. In my heart of hearts, I just want to rest. I want to get everything done, I want things to be checked off my to-do list, so I can finally relax and say I got it all done. When I worship my plans, I'm believing a lie that tells me that *in order to rest, I need to get everything done.*

Ultimately, I'm finding my worth and value (i.e., identity) in these things because I don't believe that Christ is enough. My heart isn't believing that I can rest even if I go to bed at night before crossing everything off my to-do list. My heart isn't believing that my responsibility isn't to control everything, it's to rest in the One who is IN control. I'm so thankful that God has promised to finish the work he has started in me—because I'm tired of worshiping my plans instead of worshiping the Living God.

Notes on learning to rest...

As soon as I realize my own sin, my natural reaction is not to dwell on God's holiness. I tend to dwell on all the people I've hurt as a result of my sin, how horrible I am, how far I have to go, how little I'm growing, how I'll never get better.

Once I get past that stage, I then try to fix it myself.

For example: this weekend I was reminded again how I plan and control things and then have little break downs when they don't go my way. Once I realized this and got past the "I'm such a horrible person" stage, I moved into the "fix-it" stage.

THIS IS NOT THE ANSWER. THIS IS NOT THE POINT OF GOD REVEALING MY SIN. THIS IS NOT THE GOSPEL.

Sorry for yelling. But seriously, why don't I get this? I think I will be re-learning this truth forever but this is what I've been reminded of tonight:

First, God exposing my sin is a very good thing.

Second, my guilt and "fix-it" attitudes are not good things.

Third, resting in the life, death, and resurrection of Christ in light of my sin is a very VERY good thing.

This is what I'm trying to say: when God reveals my sin, my instant pose should be on my knees before the cross, not jumping on my feet into "fix-it" action motivated by guilt.

This is so hard to do. And yet again...the answer is the gospel (isn't it always?). I need to repent of all of these newly-revealed sins and praise God that not only am I forgiven but I am considered righteous in Christ.

Resting in Christ's work on the cross is probably going to be a life-long challenge for this girl who loves to get things done and fix problems as they arise. I'm thankful that God is slowly working in my heart and teaching me that resting in His work is what my heart really needs, not a new prescription for how to fix my latest issue.

ABOUT THE AUTHOR

Ruthie Delk grew up in Belgium and graduated from Furman University in Greenville, SC with a degree in Special Education. She and her husband David live in Orlando, Florida where he is President of Man in the Mirror. David and Ruthie have three children, two of which currently reside in the "The Swamp." Go Gators!

ABOUT THE ILLUSTRATOR

Deb McCrary graduated from Houghton College with a degree in Art and Math. She has been a compulsive doodler since early childhood. While researching methods of taking lecture notes, she happily discovered visual note-taking and no longer feels guilty about doodling while she takes notes. Deb lives in Orlando, Florida, with her husband and three children.

CRAVINGGRACE.ORG

Find additional resources for your own journey or ministry to women at CravingGrace.org. You can download copies of the charts used in this book. Also, look for topics related to the Gospel 8 Diagram that cover:

- Forgiveness: The path through the pain

- Strongholds that Strangle—lies we believe and the truth that sets us free

- The Tree of Unbelief—getting to the root not the fruit

- Personal stories of women who have experienced how the gospel changes everything!

Also, you can purchase ten-packs of laminated Gospel Eight Diagrams.

Find us on Facebook at Craving Grace Like Chocolate. LIKE our page for encouraging quotes, video clips, and music that will keep you swimming in the gospel.

WWW.CRAVINGGRACE.ORG

Made in the USA
Lexington, KY
27 November 2013